D1348073

British History

(from 0 to 1945 AD)

Some other books by the author

WHO'S WHO IN SCIENCE AND TECHNOLOGY.
Scientific knowledge has been growing like yeast in bread for thousands of years. Find out about the lives and ideas of around three hundred of the brainiest brain boxes who have ever lived.
ISBN 9780750281560

WHAT THEY DON'T TELL YOU ABOUT ANCIENT GREEKS.
Did you know: the Colossus of Rhodes was nearly as big as the Statue of Liberty in New York? The Ancient Greeks really were very amazing indeed.
ISBN 9780750280501

WHAT THEY DON'T TELL YOU ABOUT ANCIENT EGYPTIANS.
The curse of Tutankhamen and why bald men smeared crocodile fat on their heads.
ISBN 9780750280495

WHAT THEY DON'T TELL YOU ABOUT ROMANS IN BRITAIN.
If modern Britain was *Roman* Britain we would worship the Queen and you could have nightingales' brains for tea.
ISBN 9780750280518

WHAT THEY DON'T TELL YOU ABOUT VIKINGS.
Blood soup, drunkenness, cruelty and courage.
ISBN9780750280488

WHAT THEY DON'T TELL YOU ABOUT ANGLO-SAXONS.
Human sacrifice, bone fights, bad monks, mad monks: how England was born.
ISBN 9780750281997

WHAT THEY DON'T TELL YOU ABOUT WORLD WAR I.
Why soldiers dug trenches - and put soap in their socks.
ISBN 9780750280464

WHAT THEY DON'T TELL YOU ABOUT WORLD WAR II.
Who won the war and why men didn't have jacket pockets.
ISBN 9780750280471

Who's Who
in
British History

(from 0 to 1945 AD)

By Bob Fowke
(with drawings by the same)

CONSULTANT Dr Miles Taylor, King's College, London

WAYLAND

a division of Hachette Children's Books

Plea for forgiveness

At least three hundred million people have lived in Britain since the year zero. Out of all these, there are less than three hundred in this book. So pity the poor author who had to do the choosing and forgive him if he's left out someone that you think should be in. In fact, if you're in a forgiving mood, you'll see that almost everyone you need to know about for your studies is included in the golden (and not so golden) three hundred.

Ask any group of people to describe an event that they've seen together and you'll get a different version from each of them. History's like that, but a thousand times worse. A lot of versions of each life have been picked over to end up with the stories described in this book. But of course each story is just *my* version. You'll have to forgive me for that too.

Bob Fowke

What other writers have said about this book

'A charming, amusing and instructive little book. I like the drawings too. I would like to give it to one of my granddaughters for her birthday.'
Christopher Hibbert.

'Informative, reliable and hugely entertaining, this is a valuable work of reference which should be not only in every school library but also in every home.'
Richard Perceval Graves.

Explorers

Sailors

Manufacturers

Doctors

How to read this book

Warriors

Pilots

Names are listed alphabetically. If you prefer to, you can find which page someone's on by looking in the index starting on page 252.

Fashion victims

Words followed by* - you can look up what they mean in the glossary starting on page 244.

Politicians and statesmen

Rebels

Sporting heroes

Names in **bold** in the text are of people who have their own entry. The little number in the margin beside them shows which page you'll find them on.

Villains

On page 249 there's a complete list of all the Prime Ministers of Great Britain.

Monarchs

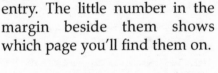

Teachers

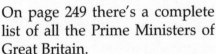

On page 250 there's a complete list of all the monarchs of Britain.

Saints

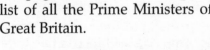

Princes

Artists

Writers

Philanthropists*

Inventors and scientists

Pretenders

Æthelred II
"Æthelred the Unready"

King who lost his kingdom
around 968-1016, KING OF ENGLAND, SAXON

During baby Æthelred's baptism he is said to have 'dirtied' the font. As a result of this bad omen, it was prophesied that Saxon England would be conquered during his reign. The prophecy was right.

He got his nickname *Unrede* ('Unready', meaning 'badly-advised') because he made so many mistakes during his reign. Of these mistakes his biggest was to try to bribe the Vikings. He ruled during a period of savage Viking attacks on England and tried to buy them off with huge sums of money, called *Danegeld*, but of course this only made them come back for more. In 1003 the Danish king himself, Svein Fork-beard, mounted a massive attack and by 1013 he had driven Æthelred out of the country. Viking Svein was now King of England.

Svein died soon after. Æthelred tried one last time to regain his crown, but died of an illness in London two years later. The Vikings had won.

Aidan, Saint

Celtic saint. Lived poor, died holy
died 651

During the Dark Ages after the fall of the Roman Empire, pagan* Saxons invaded Britain, but Christianity lingered on in the Celtic-speaking lands of Cornwall, Ireland, Wales and parts of Scotland. Aidan was a typical Celtic monk. He lived simply, any presents he was given he gave to the poor and he always travelled on foot. In 635 **Oswald** the Saxon King of Northumbria asked Aidan to convert his people to Christianity. Aidan spoke no Saxon when he arrived in Northumbria and Oswald used to translate the gentle monk's words to his Saxon warriors. King and saint became close friends.

Aidan founded a monastery at Lindisfarne (Holy Island). Lindisfarne was run simply in the Celtic style. From this remote place Christianity spread to the whole of northern England and much of the Midlands.

Aidan is said to have died leaning against a post and was buried beside the altar at Lindisfarne.

Alfred the Great

Viking basher - the greatest

849-901, KING OF WESSEX

Alfred (*elf-rede* in Saxon) means 'elf-advice'. Usually Saxon elves were mischievous, but some were friendly - including presumably those that Alfred was named after. He's the only English king to be called 'Great'.

He came to the throne of Wessex (the kingdom of the West Saxons) in 871, at a time when Viking invaders had all but conquered England. In that year he fought nine bloody battles against them. In 878 he had to hide in the marshes of Athelney in Somerset while a Viking horde rampaged through Wessex. But he fought back, forcing the Viking leader, Guthrum, to become a Christian and the rest of them to stay in Danelaw, an area controlled by the Vikings in the north-east of England. Alfred then became over-king of all England.

Far more than just a soldier, Alfred was also in many ways the father of the English language. He made sure that his nobles were educated, he himself translated important books into English and he ordered the start of the *Anglo-Saxon Chronicle*, a vital record of early English history. By the time he died, Saxon England was stronger than it had ever been, and he was loved by his people as law-giver, teacher and peace-maker.

The elves must have advised him well.

Anne

1665-1714, QUEEN OF GREAT BRITAIN (STUART)

129
238
151

Anne was a daughter of **James II**. She came to the throne after the deaths of **William III** and his wife, her sister **Mary**. Poor Anne got pregnant nineteen times but only one of her children lived past infancy.

Arkwright, Sir Richard

Energetic inventor of a spinning-frame

1732-92

Richard Arkwright started life as a humble Lancashire wigmaker and barber. He developed a new process for dying hair and by 1761 was travelling the country looking for human hair to buy. He had a lot of energy.

But hair dye was just the first of his inventions. By 1769 he'd built a machine for spinning thread (thread had been hand-spun until then). Arkwright's spinning-frame, together with his other inventions, started a revolution. Soon his machines could perform most of the processes needed for making textiles, and they could be powered by steam engines. Angry hand-workers rioted, fearful of losing their jobs. But they couldn't stop 'progress'.

Arkwright went on to build several cotton mills and ended his life with a fortune worth two and a half million pounds - a *huge* sum for those days.

Arnold, Thomas

Headmaster with vision

1795-1842

Before Thomas Arnold became Headmaster of Rugby School in 1828, English public schools were rough, tough places. There had even been riots at Rugby and Winchester and local soldiers had been brought in to keep order.

Arnold changed all that. He kept firm discipline and expelled troublemakers. And that was just the start. Until that time, pupils learned only Greek, Latin and religion; Arnold added maths, modern history, modern languages - and sport. Ex-Rugby boys began to shine at university and in the army. Soon other schools followed Arnold's example. Public schools all over the country were reformed.

His influence went even further. Baron Pierre de Coubertin was a French nobleman who admired Arnold's ideas about sport in education.
In 1886, de Coubertin had a vision while standing beside Arnold's tomb in Rugby chapel and, partly because of that vision, he went on to found the modern Olympic Games.

Arthur, 'King'

Brave soldier - the sort that myths are made of

active around 500

'King' Arthur may have been many things, but one thing he certainly *wasn't* was a king. Most likely, he was a war leader who led the Britons against invading Saxons during the Dark Ages after the fall of the Roman Empire. His name may be a nickname meaning 'Bear'.

Very little is known about the period in which he lived. (The stories about his Knights of the Round Table were made up hundreds of years later.) He is mentioned in just one book of his own time, written by an early British monk called Nennius. Nennius wrote that Arthur fought twelve battles against the Saxons. In the last and greatest of these, the Battle of Mount Badon (around 500), which may have taken place near Bath, he is said to have killed 960 Saxons. After that battle the Saxons left the British in peace for fifty years.

Arthur was later mortally wounded at the Battle of Camlaan (possibly in Wales) against his nephew Mordred, who legend says was the lover of Arthur's wife Guenevere.

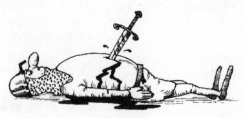

Astor, Nancy Witcher

First woman Member of Parliament

1879-1964

Born in America, Nancy Astor was beautiful, intelligent - and a woman. Beauty and intelligence were fairly rare qualities among members of parliament in 1919; being a woman was unknown.

In 1919 her second husband, Waldorf Astor, became Lord Astor and had to give up being the Member of Parliament for Sutton, in Plymouth, because lords aren't allowed to sit in the House of Commons. Nancy was elected in his place as a Conservative*. This made her the first ever woman MP to sit in the House. She was quite good at it. Among other things, she was responsible for raising the legal age for drinking alcohol to eighteen - if you think that's good.

When World War II ended in 1945, there was a general election and the Labour Party* came to power. Nancy would probably have lost her seat anyway but she decided not to stand for election - as her husband advised her. Unfortunately she then blamed her husband and they fell out. He died in 1952 but she lived on for another twelve years.

Augustine of Canterbury, Saint

Missionary to the English
- and a bit of a wimp
died 604/5

In 596, Pope Gregory the Great sent Augustine to convert the fierce, pagan* Saxons of England to Christianity. Poor Augustine was head of a nice, safe Roman monastery and he didn't want to go - but Gregory made him. Augustine and his band of forty monks landed in Kent in 597. They were met by Æthelbert, the king of Kent. Æthelbert sat outside to greet the monks because he was frightened of Christian magic - in fact both sides were frightened of each other!

Æthelbert's wife Bertha was already a Christian. She worshipped in the ruined church of St Martin's in Canterbury, a leftover from the days of the Roman Empire. So it was in Canterbury that Augustine started his mission. To this day, the top churchman in Britain is known as the 'Archbishop of Canterbury'.

King Æthelbert soon became a Christian and his subjects followed his example. Christianity rapidly spread out from Canterbury to much of Saxon England. The old savage Saxon days were almost over.

Austen, Jane

Great novelist who lived quietly

1775-1817

Miss Austen's father was a rector in the south of England. She was very good at sewing, especially satin-stitch, lived quietly with her family all her life and was popular with children ...

That might have been all anyone remembered about Jane Austen (if they remembered anything at all), if it hadn't been for one other thing - she's also one of the greatest English novelists. Her six books deal with what she knew best: the small family affairs of people of her class and time. They never deal with big themes such as war or politics. Each one is funny and clever, as she was herself. They are: *Sense and Sensibilty*, *Pride and Prejudice*, *Mansfield Park*, *Emma*, *Persuasion* and *Northanger Abbey*.

Jane never married although she's said to have fallen briefly for a gentleman she met at the seaside. She was only forty-two when she died and she's buried in Winchester Cathedral.

Bacon, Francis

Clever Tudor creep, good scientist, crafty lawyer

1561-1626

Some say that Francis Bacon was a 'boot-licker', being the humble adviser first of **Elizabeth I** and then of **James I**. Others say that he was a great thinker. Both opinions are probably correct.

Francis Bacon was one of the cleverest men of his time and rose to become Lord Chancellor of England under James I. But on the way he brought to trial his former ally the **Earl of Essex**, although Essex had once been very generous to him, giving him both land and friendship. And in 1618 he also tried the great Tudor hero, **Sir Walter Raleigh**. Both his victims had their heads chopped off.

On the other hand, he helped science by insisting on the importance of experiments to prove ideas. In fact he died because of an experiment: he caught cold while stuffing a chicken with snow so as to see the effect of cold in preserving the flesh.

Bacon, Roger
"Friar Bacon"

Marvellous medieval mind

around 1220-1294

The pig is said to be an intelligent animal. Bacon was no pig, although you might think so from his name, but he was certainly very intelligent.

Roger Bacon was one of the most brilliant men of the Middle Ages. He was the first person to suggest that people could sail round the world, he invented magnifying glasses and was once thought to have invented gunpowder as well. He believed that ideas should be proved with experiments whenever possible, and in this he was way ahead of his time. Condemned by the leader of the Franciscan Order of Friars around 1257, of which he was a member (hence his nickname 'Friar Bacon'), he was imprisoned for ten years. Luckily for him, he won the support of Pope Clement IV and was finally freed. It was for Clement that he wrote his most important work, *Opus Maius*.

But popes don't live for ever, and the Church was out to silence him. *Opus Maius* wasn't published until 1733 - 439 years after his death.

Baden-Powell,
Robert Stephenson Smyth

Founder of the Scouts - he did his best!

1857-1941

Robert Baden-Powell loved the outdoors. As a boy he went camping with his brothers in the school holidays. Later he scouted (went ahead to get advance information) for the army, earning the title *Impeesa* or 'The Wolf That Never Sleeps' for night-scouting duties in Matabeleland in East Africa during 1896.

Baden-Powell led the British defence during the Siege of Mafeking - 217 blood-soaked days of the second Boer War (1899-1902). Returning from Africa a national hero, he was amazed to find that one of his army books *Aids to Scouting* was being widely used by teachers in boys' schools. He rewrote it as a proper children's book and by 1908, boy scout troops had sprung up all over the country. Soon there were Boy Scouts all over the world. They were followed later by Girl Guide Troops and by the Cubs and Brownies for younger children.

During a grand Jamboree or International Scout Meeting in 1920 Baden-Powell was named 'Chief Scout of the World'. This was probably his proudest title - more so than 'Lieutenant General' or 'Baron', which he also became.

Baird, John Logie

Pioneer of TV - watch this tea-chest!

1888-1946

Baird was a Scottish engineer who started off trying to make and sell socks, jam, honey and soap. His ideas were good, but he had to break off each new business venture due to ill health.

In 1922, after a nervous breakdown, Baird moved to Hastings, determined to develop the first ever television. His first attempt was a crazy contraption: the lamp was mounted in a biscuit tin, the motor in a tea-chest and the whole thing was stuck together with knitting needles, sealing wax and string. But by 1924, he'd transmitted the world's first ever television image over several feet. It was a picture of a Maltese cross. He then moved to London, struggling against sickness and poverty, but in 1926 - success at last! He showed his mad contraption to fifty scientists - the first demonstration of a television. By 1928, he'd transmitted pictures between London and New York.

Up until 1932, when the BBC took over, all television in England was provided by the Baird Television Development Company. Ever inventive, Baird experimented with colour, big screens and stereoscopic effects until his death, aged fifty-eight in 1946.

Barnardo, Thomas John

Founder of Dr Barnardo's Homes and seriously good Victorian

1845-1905

Thomas Barnardo's first job was as clerk in a wine merchant's office in Dublin - a poor choice of job since he didn't like drinking and soon hated the evils of drink. At seventeen he was already a serious Christian, spending all his spare time preaching or visiting the poor in the Dublin slums.

In 1866 Barnardo moved to London to train to be a missionary to China. He was horrified by the number of poor children on London's streets and began to work part-time for a 'ragged school'. The poor children so touched his heart that he changed his mind about going to China. In 1870, he opened his first 'home', a house for homeless boys in Stepney in London. His ideas about children's homes spread like wildfire and before long there were Dr Barnardo's Homes all over Britain and Canada.

By the time of his death, he had rescued 59,384 homeless children from poverty and helped another 250,000. His homes boasted: 'no destitute child ever refused admission'. They meant it.

Becket, Thomas à
"Saint Thomas"

Medieval Archbishop with a mind of his own
around 1118-1170

115 As young men, Thomas à Becket and **Henry II** were as close as peas in a pod. They fought side by side and were the best of friends. Thomas was a brave fighter who once unhorsed a French knight in single combat.

In 1162 King Henry made Thomas Archbishop of Canterbury - which turned out to be a big mistake from Henry's point of view. Thomas took his new job very seriously and from then on disagreed with Henry almost whenever he felt like it. Quarrels between friends are often the bitterest and Thomas had to flee to France. When he returned, he was attacked by four knights who claimed to have come in the King's name. After a struggle inside Canterbury Cathedral the top of his head was struck off and he died.

Thomas the Martyr became England's most famous saint. Thousands visited his shrine at Canterbury every year.

Bede
"The Venerable Bede"

Saxon historian - this book wouldn't be the same without him

672/3-735

In 680, after an outbreak of plague, just two monks who could read were left alive in the monastery of Jarrow in the north-east of England: the Abbot and a seven-year-old boy. The Abbot and the little boy took turns to sing the services until the other survivors learned their parts.

The boy was Bede. Even at seven he was on his way to being a scholar, studying Latin, Greek, Hebrew, medicine, astronomy and singing. He made use of all this learning in later life, in particular in his most famous book: *The Ecclesiastical History of the English People*. It tells the story of the Anglo-Saxons from their coming to Britain around 450 up to Bede's own day.

The Venerable Bede, as he's known, spent all his life in Jarrow, but by the time he died his fame had spread throughout Europe. In fact, he only moved after his death - when his bones were stolen and taken to Durham Cathedral.

Black Prince *see* **Edward III**

Blackbeard *see* **Teach, Captain Edward**

Blake, William

Visionary artist and poet - a bit weird

1757-1827

William Blake saw visions: he was once nearly beaten by his father for claiming to have seen a tree filled with angels. He was also a republican* and one of the few people in London to wear the red 'cap of liberty' while the French Revolution was going on. He was a bit odd really. A friend told of seeing Blake and his wife naked in their garden, like Adam and Eve.

Blake trained as an engraver in London and lived mainly by working for booksellers. But his greatest work came from his own visions and poems. The first such work was a little book called *Songs of Innocence*. He printed it himself using his own technique, writing backwards onto the printing plates so that the words came out right in the prints.

He never stopped working, once telling a friend 'I don't understand what you mean by 'want [lack] of a holiday''. He was still working when he died in poverty in London, where he'd spent nearly all his life.

Booth, William
" General Booth "

Founder of the Salvation Army and very good Victorian do-gooder

1829-1912

William Booth was the son of a poor Nottingham builder. As a result of his poor childhood he wanted to help those even worse off than himself - and there were a lot of them in Victorian England. When still only a teenager he became a passionate Christian and a rousing preacher. He joined the Methodists but split with them in 1861 to form his own Christian Mission dedicated to saving souls and to helping the poor.

In 1878 the Christian Mission changed its name to the Salvation Army. Military titles and uniforms soon followed (although Booth was never very keen on them). Of course the Salvation Army was never remotely like a real army. Far from killing people, it worked very hard to help them - and still does. Salvation Army hostels all over the country give shelter to thousands of homeless and desperate people.

Boudicca

Bold British freedom fighter against Roman rule

died 60, BRITISH QUEEN

Boudicca, a large, frightening woman with red hair, was the wife of King Prasutagus of the Iceni, a British tribe based in modern East Anglia. On his death King Prasutagus left his great wealth jointly to the Roman Emperor Claudius and to his daughters, hoping to save some of it from the Romans who had recently invaded Britain. Fat hope - Roman officials beat his wife, assaulted his daughters and tried to take the lot.

Under Boudicca's leadership, the Iceni rose in revolt. They laid waste London, St Albans and Colchester, killing 70,000 Romans and taking no prisoners or slaves. It was the most serious of all British rebellions against the Romans. The Roman governor, Suetonius Paulinus, hurried south from Anglesey where he had been busy smashing the Druids. He defeated Boudicca somewhere in the Midlands. Nearly 80,000 Britains were killed and Boudicca herself took poison.

Boyle, Robert

Discoverer of 'Boyle's Law'

1627-91

Robert Boyle was a boy wonder. By the time he was eight he could speak Greek and Latin. When only ten he used algebra to calm himself when he got upset. And by the time he was fourteen he was studying the works of the great Italian scientist, Galileo.

He grew up to be a founder member of the Royal Society* (1660). The motto of the Royal Society was *'nullis in verba'*, meaning broadly, 'don't accept someone's word alone' - in other words, 'test scientific theories by experiment'. That's exactly what Boyle did. Through experimentation he discovered Boyle's Law, which states that the pressure of a given quantity of gas varies inversely to its volume at a constant temperature. He also proved that sound cannot carry through a vacuum and that a feather and a stone will fall at the same speed in a vacuum.

Boyle refused to be made a lord or a vicar, even though he was very religious. He died unmarried claiming never to have been 'hurt by Cupid'.

Brendan, Saint
"the Navigator"

Early Irish explorer - subject of travellers' tales

around 485-578

Brendan was brought up by a woman saint called Ita, in Limerick in Ireland. Perhaps because of her influence he became a priest. But despite being a priest, he always had a restless soul and longed to discover 'the mysterious land far from human ken' which he'd seen in a vision.

He probably made two voyages into the unknown. He may well have got as far as Iceland, and some say he discovered America. Before going on his second voyage Ita advised him to build a wooden ship and not to try again in a leaky, leather boat like last time. He set sail with sixty companions in a wooden ship well stocked with herbs and seeds.

Many legends grew up around his travels but it's impossible to know how many, if any, of them are true - for instance, the 'giant fish' he saw might have been a whale. Be that as it may, Brendan the Navigator lived to be ninety-four years old, an incredible age for that time - so one incredible thing is true anyway.

Brontë, Anne *see* **Brontë, Charlotte**

Brontë, Charlotte

Good writer, good sisters, bad brother

1816-55

Charlotte spent most of her life in her father's remote vicarage of Haworth in Yorkshire with her two sisters Emily and Anne, and her brother Bramwell. The Reverend Brontë was a strange man who used to fire pistols from the back door when upset and fed his children on potatoes without meat so as to toughen them up.

During their childhood, the three sisters filled the long hours by writing - when she was ten, Charlotte filled 22 books of 100 pages each. All three grew up to become writers. Their best-known books are *Jane Eyre* by Charlotte, *Wuthering Heights* by Emily and *The Tenant of Wildfell Hall* by Anne.

Bramwell was a bit useless and failed as an artist. He died in September 1848. Emily soon followed him, dying that December, and Anne died the following May. Only Charlotte lived on. She even got married but sadly died a year later in 1855. Her husband Mr Nicholls and the Reverend Brontë lived on alone in the vicarage.

Brontë, Emily Jane *see* **Brontë, Charlotte**

Bruce, Robert I
"Robert the Bruce"

Good king - and Scottish freedom fighter

1274-1329, KING OF SCOTLAND

75   In 1296, the mighty English king, **Edward I, Hammer of the Scots**, invaded Scotland. He declared that there would be no more kings in Scotland.

224   Some Scots thought differently. **William Wallace** led the fight for independence. For a while Robert the Bruce, then Earl of Carrick, stayed loyal to the English King but, after Wallace was executed in 1305, Robert took over the Scottish leadership. In 1306, he was crowned Robert I of Scotland by his followers. But he still had to fight for his kingdom - he spent time on the run and is said to have learned patience while hiding in a cave and watching a spider spin its web. His luck turned in 1307
76   when Edward I died. Edward's son, **Edward II**, was a weak king and Robert defeated him at the Battle of Bannockburn in 1314. Almost 30,000 of the English army died in that battle.

Robert's crown was now safe. From then until his death from leprosy he ruled wisely and well.

Brummell, George Bryan
" Beau Brummell "

Dandy dresser and Regency fashion-setter

1778-1840

Beau (it means 'handsome' in French) Brummell got his nickname because he was always very neatly and fashionably dressed, even as a schoolboy. It was while he was at Eton in fact that he became friends with the then Prince of Wales, later **George IV**.

Beau became a leader of fashion. It's said the Prince once cried when told that Beau didn't like the cut of his coat. Beau was also known for his witty remarks. On seeing the (very fat) Prince at a party, he is said to have remarked to the Prince's companion: 'Who's your fat friend?' - which isn't the sort of thing you're meant to say about a prince. (This was *after* he'd fallen out with the Prince - probably because of something else he'd said.)

In 1816 he fled to France to avoid going to prison for gambling debts. He never returned to England, dying in France twenty-four years later.

98

Brunel, Isambard Kingdom

Victorian engineer - he built to last

1806-59

Isambard Brunel was a hard worker. When helping his father, Marc Brunel, in the construction of the first tunnel under the Thames in 1826, he once worked for ninety-six hours in one go.

Isambard Brunel is most famous for his work on the *Great Western Railway*, especially for building the Royal Albert Bridge to carry trains across the River Tamar in Plymouth, and for his ships. He understood that larger ships need less power per ton than smaller ships (this is because their surface area is smaller in relation to their total volume). So he designed the massive *Great Western* which crossed the Atlantic four days faster than its rival *The Sirius* which was half its size. Following this he built the *Great Britain*, the first large ship to be driven by screw propellers. (It's now a floating museum in the docks of Bristol.)

His biggest ship was *The Great Eastern* which was designed to be large enough to sail to Australia without refuelling. It was overwork on *The Great Eastern* which probably killed him. His health broke down on the day of her first trial voyage and he died ten days later.

Bunyan John

Powerful Puritan* preacher who wrote *Pilgrim's Progress*

1628-88

As a young man John Bunyan loved dancing and swearing, but when he was sixteen his mother died, his father remarried, and John angrily joined the Parliamentary Army. Shortly after, a friend who'd asked to take his place in a fight was shot in the head with a musket ball. Shocked, Bunyon got married, read two religious books belonging to his young wife and turned seriously Christian.

Bunyan took to preaching, at a time when unauthorized preaching was illegal. Accused of being a 'witch, a Jesuit and a highwayman' among other things, he spent the next twelve years in Bedford County Jail. In or out of jail he never stopped preaching - or writing. From his third book *Sighs from Hell or the Groans of a Damned Soul* to his most famous *Pilgrim's Progress*, his writing is always clear and powerful. *Pilgrim's Progress* describes the amazing journey of a man called Christian in search of religious salvation.

Bunyan died after preaching in London at the age of sixty. Earlier that day he'd ridden all the way from Reading in heavy rain.

Burton, Sir Richard Francis

Vigorous Victorian voyager to various places

1821-90

As a child Burton learned six languages or dialects and the use of a sword, while his rich parents travelled from place to place round Europe. He soaked up languages like a sponge. As well as European languages, he later learned Hindi, Gujerati, Sindhi, Punjabi, Farsi, Arabic, Sanskrit and Pushtu, oh and Camoen, which is spoken in Goa. He learned most of these while serving as a soldier in India.

His first major journey of exploration was to Mecca disguised as a Muslim (1853), but he was so widely travelled and had so many adventures that it's impossible to list them all here. He's especially famous for his journey with **John Hanning Speke** to discover the source of the Nile (1856-9), and for his translation of the *Arabian Nights* into English.

After he died, his body was placed in a stone coffin inside a marble mausoleum built to look like an Arab tent, in the Roman Catholic* cemetery at Mortlake in London. His wife's coffin was later placed beside him.

Byrd, William

Famous composer

1543-1623

William Byrd wrote music as sweet as birdsong. He was taught his trade by the great composer **Thomas Tallis** and worked at the court of **Elizabeth I**.

214
85

Byron, George Gordon
"Lord Byron"

Handsome poet with a limp

1788-1824

Lord Byron was the world's first media megastar. When his long poem *Childe Harold* came out in 1813 it sold in huge numbers. 'I woke one morning and found myself famous' as he put it. The poem was based on his travels in Greece, the country to which he returned at the end of his life.

Byron was very handsome. The fact that he was slightly lame only made him *more* attractive to women. In 1815, he married, but it was a bad choice - he and his wife soon quarrelled bitterly. In the scandal of their separation, he had to leave England and moved to Italy, where he was friends with the poet **Shelley** and where he wrote another long poem, *Don Juan*.

In 1823 he sailed to Greece, carrying arms and soldiers for the Greek War of Independence from Turkey. He's still a national hero to the Greeks. He died of a fever at the Greek fort of Missolonghi on 18 April 1824.

Cabot, Sebastian

Map-maker and merchant

around **1476-1557**

In the spring of 1497 two small ships set sail from Bristol. Their leader was John Cabot, an Italian who had settled in England. With him probably went his three sons. By March they had landed in Newfoundland - the first modern Europeans to 'discover' North America.

The second of John Cabot's sons, Sebastian, never discovered anything quite that important again, although he did manage an expedition to Brazil for the King of Spain and following that he made a famous map of the world. His biggest success came in 1551 when the Merchant Adventurers' Company was founded, with Sebastian as its governor. Its aim was to find a north-east passage round Russia for trade with China. Although they never found the north-east passage, they did start English trade with Russia. Sebastian was governor of the company until his death.

Cadbury, George

Model village maker

1839-1922

Yes, *Cadbury* as in 'Cadbury's Chocolate'. George and his brother Richard took over their father's Birmingham-based chocolate business when their father died in 1899. The family were Quakers* and strictly religious. George himself never drank alcohol or smoked tobacco. When young he avoided tea, coffee and newspapers as well.

The Cadburys always cared for their workers. (They ate breakfast with them every working day.) In 1879 when they moved their factory to a new site at Bournville to the south of Birmingham, George saw the chance to improve the workers' lives. He built a 'model' village of three hundred houses around the new factory. 'Model' meant that it was a good example of how such a village should be and therefore worth copying. For instance, every house had a garden. It set a high standard for working class housing.

George kept up the good work. Until the age of seventy-two he used to cycle into the centre of Birmingham every Sunday to give Bible classes and teach working men to read.

Caratacus

British 'king' who resisted the Romans

active around 50-100

Caratacus (sometimes called Caractacus) and his brother Togodumnus were sons of Cunobelin, king of the Trinobantes and the most powerful king in Britain at the time of the Roman invasion in 43. The Roman Emperor Claudius led the capture of Camulodunum, Cunobelin's capital. Togodumnus was killed around this time, but Caratacus escaped to south Wales where he fought back against the Romans for nine bitter years.

He was finally defeated at a battle somewhere in Shropshire in the summer of 50. His wife, daughters and other brothers were captured, but he himself fled north, to the territory of the Brigantes (modern Lancashire and Cumbria). Not that it did him any good - Cartimandua (means 'Sleek Filly'), the Queen of the Brigantes, handed him over to the Romans. He and his family were taken to Rome to be paraded through the streets. The crowds admired his bravery during this ordeal and his life was spared. He lived on in Rome for another four years, so legend says.

Carroll, Lewis
(real name: Charles Lutwidge Dodgson)

Classic kids' writer and pioneer of photography

1832-98

Lewis Carroll was a lecturer in mathematics at Oxford University. He was the author of *Alice's Adventures in Wonderland* and *Through the Looking Glass and What Alice Found There*, two amazing children's books. His best 'serious' book about mathematics was *Euclid and his Modern Rivals* (1879) - which many readers refused to take seriously because it was full of jokes! As well as being a mathematician and writer, he was also a pioneer photographer.

Alice in Wonderland came from stories he told to Alice Liddell and her sisters (the daughters of the Dean of his Oxford college) during a boat trip one sunny afternoon in 1862. Carroll was shy with adults and had a stammer. He was able to talk to children far more easily.

Casement, Sir Roger David

Traitor - or Irish freedom fighter

1864-1916

Roger Casement came from a Protestant* Northern Ireland family. He travelled in Africa and worked as British Consul in various African countries. In 1911 he was knighted after nineteen years of distinguished service and shortly afterwards retired to Ireland.

Then began his other career. At that time all of Ireland was still united with Britain. Yet Casement was a fierce believer in total Irish independence. When World War I started, he went to Germany to try to get German help against the British. In return he tried to persuade Irish prisoners of war to fight for the Germans. By 1916, he'd arranged for a shipload of German arms to be sent to Dublin for the planned 'Easter Rising'. The British Government got wind of this plan. Casement, who had travelled to Ireland in a German submarine, was arrested, taken to London and charged with high treason. He was hanged in Pentonville Prison on 3 August 1916.

Catherine of Aragon

First wife of Henry VIII - poor thing

1485-1536, QUEEN OF ENGLAND

120 This is a tale of marriages that were and marriages that weren't. Catherine of Aragon and **Henry VIII** were married when she was twenty-four and he was eighteen, but first …

119 In 1487 when Catherine was two, **Henry VII** asked her parents, Philip and Isabella of Spain, if she could marry his son Arthur. They duly got married in 1501 - but Arthur died a year later. What was Catherine to do next? There was even talk of her marrying Henry VII who had recently lost his own wife, Arthur's mother. In the end she married Arthur's brother Henry VIII in 1509 (but not before *he'd* tried to marry her sister Juan, Queen of Castile, who was mad as a hatter).

All went well with Catherine and Henry's marriage for years, although four of their children died as babies and
150 only the future Queen **Mary** survived. Then Henry
24 tired of her. He wanted to marry **Anne Boleyn**. He said that a widow couldn't marry her brother-in-law. So, as Catherine had once been married to Arthur, she and Henry had never been married in the first place! The Pope was on Catherine's side and refused to end their marriage, so Henry started the Church of England with himself as its head. He married Anne Boleyn in 1533. Catherine died shortly after that, of cancer probably - but perhaps also of sadness.

Cavell, Edith Louisa

World War I heroine and nurse

1865-1915

Edith Cavell was a pioneering English nurse who went to Belgium in 1906 to help train Belgian nurses. She was the first matron of a well-known clinic in Brussels and when World War I started in 1914, she was left in charge of it. When the Germans captured Brussels later that year, they let her carry on working - she cared for Germans as well as everyone else.

Meanwhile many British and Belgian soldiers had been cut off by the German advance. They tried to hide as best they could, but if found by the Germans they were shot. Belgian farmers helped many to escape - as did Edith. But in less than a year, the Germans found out what she was up to and arrested her. She was found guilty of helping enemy soldiers to escape and the Germans shot her. At that time the British never executed women spies and they thought her execution was cold-blooded murder.

Cavendish, Henry

Weird scientist who was frightened of women

1731-1810

Henry Cavendish was a mad professor. He hated talking and if he had to talk he never talked to more than one man at a time and never *ever* to women. He was so frightened of women that he gave all orders to his maid servants in written messages and sacked any maid who came near him. He lived for science and died alone.

He hardly even cared whether people found out about his discoveries - almost none of his work on electricity was published during his lifetime. His method for testing the strength of an electric current was to shock himself. Working alone he discovered hydrogen and that water was made of two gases (hydrogen and oxygen as we now know them). Later he discovered what is known as the 'gravitational constant' and, from that, the mass of the earth. The Cavendish Laboratories in Cambridge University are named after him.

Caxton, William

First English printer

around 1422-1491

As a London cloth merchant or 'mercer' trading in Bruges (in what is now Belgium), William Caxton was in touch with new developments in Europe. He always claimed that he learned the art of printing so as to make copies of a book he'd translated from French into English and 'to prevent idleness', as he put it. Having learned printing at Cologne, he printed this book (called *The Recuyell* [record] *of the Historyes of Troye*) in Bruges in 1474 - the very first book to be printed in English. In 1476, he moved back to London and set up his printing press at Westminster. Over the next fourteen years he printed nearly eighty different books. It was the start of a revolution.

Shortly before his death he printed a small book, *The Art and Craft how to die*. Perhaps he knew that his own time was near.

Cecil, Robert *see* Cecil, William

Cecil, William

Top Tudor adviser to Elizabeth I

1520-98

William Cecil was one of England's greatest statesmen. He had a genius for running things - especially the country. He was senior counsellor to all three of **Henry VIII's** children: **Edward VI, Mary** and **Elizabeth I**. He was Elizabeth's closest adviser for forty years.

120
79,
150,
85

During Mary's reign he briefly became a Catholic but, horrified by her cruelty, he soon contacted her sister, the future Elizabeth I. When Mary died Elizabeth asked him to be her chief adviser. She told him: 'This judgement I have of you, that you will not be corrupted by any manner of gifts.' She was right - although he did spend a lot of money on his houses: Theobalds, Cecil House and Burghley. (He was made Baron Burghley by Elizabeth in 1571.)

When William died his son Robert took his place. It was Robert who arranged for **James VI** of Scotland to become King of both Scotland and England on Elizabeth's death in 1603. He was a brilliant, quietly-spoken hunchback who liked gambling and dinner parties. He was good fun. His parrot liked to dance on the dinner table!

128

Chamberlain, Joseph

Local government reformer

1836-1914

Joseph Chamberlain was a reformer and Birmingham was what he reformed. He did more to change that city than anyone else before or since. By the time he'd finished, it had gas works for gas lighting, a sewage farm, some decent workers' housing and was on the way to having free libraries and an art gallery. It was Chamberlain who started the reforms in local government throughout Britain.

In 1876 he became a liberal member of parliament and a national politician. And then in 1889 Prime Minister Salisbury made him Secretary of State for the Colonies. Chamberlain believed that the British Empire was good for the people it ruled over, so he worked hard to make it stronger and more united until his retirement in 1906.

He died, as he would have wished - in Birmingham.

Charles Edward Louis Philip Casimir
" Bonnie Prince Charlie"

Catholic pretender to the throne of Great Britain

1720-88

Charles Edward, Bonnie Prince Charlie, was known as the Young Pretender, his father was the Old Pretender, and his grandfather was **James II** who'd been forced to leave the throne of England in 1688. They were all Stuarts*, they were all Roman Catholics*, and they all believed that they were the rightful rulers of Britain.

In August 1745, Charles decided to win back the crown for his family. He landed in Scotland and the highland clans rushed to join him. With his Scottish army he marched south, reaching as far as Derby in the Midlands. But the English refused to join him and he had to retreat. His bedraggled army was smashed to pieces at Culloden Moor in April 1746. The bodies of his highland soldiers were piled three or four deep after the ferocious battle.

Charles himself was hunted through Scotland for several months before escaping to France. He died a drunkard in Italy, deserted by his wife whom he had mistreated - he was never very 'Bonnie' anyway.

Charles I

Only king to get the chop

1600-49, KING OF ENGLAND, SCOTLAND AND IRELAND (STUART)

Charles I's head was chopped off outside Whitehall on 30 January 1649. He's the only king of England and Scotland to have been executed, although many have died violent deaths.

His troubles started almost from the moment he was crowned in 1625. Many members of the House of Commons no longer believed that monarchs should have total (absolute) power. The Puritans* among them suspected him of favouring Catholics. Parliament refused to vote him taxes and for eleven years he tried to rule without any parliament at all - until he ran out of money. Things came to a head in 1642 when he marched to Parliament with an armed gang of followers and tried to arrest five members who were speaking against him. He lost the civil war that followed, falling into the hands of the Puritan Parliamentary army in 1647.

The Commons accused Charles of 'levying war against the Parliament and Kingdom of England'. He refused to plead his innocence, saying they had no right to try him in the first place, since he was their king. He probably knew he was going to die anyway.

Charles II

Merry monarch who liked to live well

1630-85, KING OF ENGLAND, SCOTLAND AND IRELAND (STUART)

48 Charles II fought for his father **Charles I** during the Civil War (1642-51) between king and Protestant* Parliament. After his father was executed, Charles II was
62 defeated by **Oliver Cromwell** at the Battle of Worcester, spending the next forty-one days in disguise and on the run. It was after the Battle of Worcester that he's said to have hidden in an oak tree while his enemies searched for him below. He finally escaped to France. For the rest of his life he loved to tell stories of his exciting adventures on the run.

Nine years later his fortunes changed: he landed at Dover in May 1661 and was crowned shortly after. He pardoned all his enemies except those who had sentenced his father to death. He loved to live well and had at least thirteen mistresses, including the beautiful actress Nell Gwyn. Just before he died he admitted that he'd become a Roman Catholic* after all - and asked the country to look after Nell.

Chatham, Earl of *see* **Pitt, William**

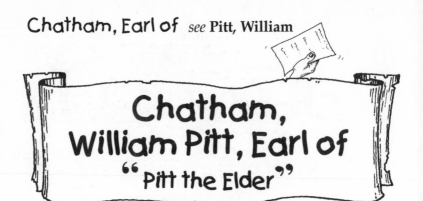

Chatham, William Pitt, Earl of
"Pitt the Elder"

Powerful prime minister who built the first British Empire

1708-78

For much of the eighteenth century Britain and France were locked in a struggle for world power. It was due to William Pitt more than anyone else that Britain came out on top.

1756 saw the start of the Seven Years War (1756-63) which was part of that struggle. **George II** wanted the British army to wage war in Europe. He loathed Pitt who wanted to fight overseas. Tall and strong, Pitt was a brilliant and overwhelming speaker (when he was speaking, you could hear his voice *outside* Parliament). He drove the country to victory after victory. 1759 is called the 'Year of Victories' because there were so many British triumphs. People said that London's bells were worn out with ringing. By 1763, Britain dominated most of India and North America - and the British Empire had been born.

Pitt lived on, in and out of power. He died after collapsing during a speech in the House of Lords against Britain's toffee-nosed behaviour towards her American colonists.

Chaucer, Geoffrey

Writer of *The Canterbury Tales*

around 1343-1400

Geoffrey Chaucer is a giant among English writers. It's mainly because of Chaucer that the southern English of his day grew into our modern written language. The son of a London wine merchant, he spent much of his life working for **Edward III**. He fought in Edward's army in France, he went on missions to France and Italy for him and he became his controller of customs, in fact a civil servant.

Chaucer wrote in English, not French or Latin as was common at the time. His greatest work, *The Canterbury Tales*, is a collection of stories told by a group of pilgrims on their way to Canterbury. Chaucer took his characters from the rough, tough world around him and his tales are a window on that world. Even today, six hundred years later, they're still good to read, if the words are modernized in places.

Churchill, John, first Duke of Marlborough

Military genius who thrashed the French

1650-1722

John Churchill was supreme commander of the Dutch and British forces during the War of the Spanish Succession (1701-14) against France. He was very handsome and daring and was perhaps the most brilliant British general ever, crushing the French in four famous battles: Blenheim (1704), Ramillies (1706), Oudenarde (1708) and Malplaquet (1709). In thanks for his services Parliament built Blenheim Palace in Oxfordshire for him.

His career was both helped and hindered by his very clever wife, Sarah. Sarah dominated the court of her close friend Queen **Anne** for many years. But she was an incredibly bad-tempered and quarrelsome woman and fell out with the Queen as she did with everyone. In old age after John had died, she used to tell, with tears in her eyes, how she once cut off her hair to annoy him. He seemed to take no notice at the time - but she found the locks wrapped up in a drawer after his death.

Churchill, Sir Winston Leonard Spencer

World War II leader

1874-1965

Churchill was often drawn as a bulldog in cartoons - with good reason. Like a bulldog, he was stubborn and aggressive with a short neck. He needed to be: without Churchill's leadership Britain would never have stood up to the Nazis in the Second World War. Unlike a bulldog, he smoked cigars, drank champagne for lunch and was a brilliant writer.

He started out as a soldier, fighting in the Battle of Omdurman in the Sudan in 1898. The next year he was captured by the Boers during the Boer War in South Africa but escaped. But politics was always his passion. As President of the Board of Trade in 1908, he helped 145 **Lloyd George** put in place the first state pensions, health and unemployment schemes. Later, during the First World War, he was responsible for a disastrous expedition to the Dardanelles in modern Turkey, after which he returned to being a soldier and fought in the trenches in France. His moment of glory came in 1940 when he was chosen to be Prime Minister in the war against Nazi Germany. Whatever else he may have done or failed to do, his leadership in that war made him a national hero.

Clive, Lord Robert
" Clive of India"

Military genius who started British rule in India

1725-74

Robert Clive was always brave as a lion and lucky with it - an angry Frenchman once took a shot at him. Clive, previously wounded, was slumped between two men at the time - the bullet killed both of them but never touched him!

At eighteen he went out to India to work as a clerk in a merchant's office - and hated it. When war broke out between the French and English and their local allies, he was quick to join the fighting. At the siege of Arcot in 1751, he and his troop of 500 held out against 10,000 Frenchmen and Indians. His greatest triumph was at the Battle of Plassey in 1757, when his force of 3000 defeated a French/Indian army of 55,000.

After Plassey the British became the real rulers of India. Clive was made a lord and became a wealthy member of parliament. Sadly, he had bouts of depression and was addicted to opium. Sick and in pain, he killed himself after another stay in India.

Cnut

Viking invader who grabbed England but ruled wisely

died 1035, KING OF ENGLAND, DENMARK AND NORWAY, DANISH

Cnut, also called Canute or Knut, was the son of Svein Fork-beard, Viking king of Denmark. Born a pagan*, he was baptised a Christian around 1000, although Christianity didn't change his Viking habits. He sailed with Fork-beard to conquer England in 1013, forcing the English king **Æthelred the Unready** to flee the country. Fork-beard died in 1014 and Cnut was chosen by the Viking fleet to be king of England. The English resisted and Æthelred returned. This time it was Cnut's turn to flee - but not before he'd cut off the hands, ears and noses of his English hostages.

He was back again soon enough. By 1016 he'd defeated **Edmund II Ironside**, Æthelred's successor, and when Edmund died a year later, Cnut was chosen to be King of all England. He settled down to rule peacefully, marrying Æthelred's widow Emma as a gesture of peace to the English. A famous story describes how he had his chair placed in the waves in order to show that only God controls the tides - not he, Cnut, as used to be thought. By the time of his death he had given England seventeen years of peace and had become King of Denmark and Norway as well.

Coleridge, Samuel Taylor *see* **Wordsworth, William**

Columba, Saint

Missionary to Scotland
around 521-597

Columba was Irish, the son of an Irish chieftain. That is to say - he was a *Scot*. It's confusing: the Irish used to be called 'Scots' and they gave their name to 'Scotland' when they invaded it during the Dark Ages at the fall of the Roman Empire. Later they stopped being called 'Scots' and were called Irish instead. So Columba, a Scot, took Christianity from Ireland to 'Scotland'.

Columba may have been sent to Scotland as a punishment for fighting in a battle in 561 - priests weren't meant to fight in battles. Be that as it may, in 563 he started a monastery on the island of Iona off the west Scottish coast. From there he converted the barbarian 'Picts' (who lived in the north-west of Scotland) to Christianity. It was from the monastery at Iona that 7 **Saint Aidan** left to convert the Saxons of northern England one hundred years later.

Constable, John

Landscape painter - pity about the weather

1776-1837

When the painter Fuseli (1741-1825) said that Constable's paintings made him 'call for my great coat and umbrella', he didn't mean that he wanted to leave the room. He meant that Constable was very good at painting the English landscape - and English weather!

John Constable was the son of a wealthy Suffolk mill owner. He always loved the flat Suffolk countryside and loved to paint the Suffolk fields, mills and skies. His fresh, honest paintings of everyday scenes were very different to the grand Italian landscapes which were then fashionable - so different that he didn't sell a single painting to anyone except friends or family until he was thirty-eight! Fortunately the French loved his work. It was a Frenchman who first bought his most famous painting *The Haywain*. Later the English learned to love him too and now he's one of the most famous of all English painters.

Cook, James
" Captain Cook "

Explorer who 'discovered' Australia

1728-79

Captain Cook was a brave sailor who charted the coasts of Australia and New Zealand among many other places. The son of a poor Yorkshire farm worker, he started to work for a Whitby shipowner when he was eighteen, sailing the North Sea in stout, sturdy coal-hauling barques. While the ships were laid up for winter, as was the custom, he learned mathematics for navigation. It was perfect training for an explorer.

In 1755, he joined the navy and rose to be master of his own ship. He mapped the coastline of Newfoundland (1763-8) and in 1768 was asked to command an expedition to the Pacific to observe the transit of the planet Venus (similar to an eclipse - needed by scientists to work out longitude for navigation) and to look for Australia. He chose to sail in *The Endeavour*, a coal-hauling barque such as he'd known in his youth - and tough enough for unknown seas. On this long voyage (1768-71) he found Tahiti and New Zealand among other places - and Australia.

He was killed by the Tahitians in a quarrel over a stolen boat during his third voyage (1776-9).

Cranmer, Thomas

Tudor bishop who wrote the Prayer Book - and burned

1489-1556

120
41
Thomas Cranmer was a Protestant*. He helped **Henry VIII** to divorce his first wife, the Catholic* **Catherine of Aragon**, against the wishes of the Pope. As Archbishop of Canterbury he agreed that Henry could be the Supreme Head of the Church of England instead of the Pope. Later he was in charge of the first prayer book of the Church of England, which is beautifully written.

150
Sometime after Henry's death, Catherine of Aragon's daughter, the Catholic Queen **Mary** came to the throne. Cranmer was sentenced to burn at the stake in Oxford. But first he was 'degraded': stripped of all his bishop's robes and his hair cropped short. In fear of death he signed six 'admissions' agreeing that the Pope was head of the Church of England after all. That was the low point of his life.

On the day of his death, he took back all his 'admissions' and ran to the stake so fast that others could hardly keep up with him. Once the flames were lit, he put the hand which had done the signing into them saying: 'This hand has offended'. He died bravely.

Crippen, Hawley, Harvey

He chopped up the body

1862-1910

Crippen was an American who studied medicine and came to live in London in 1896. His wife was a failed opera singer. He murdered her, cut up her body, burned the bones and buried the rest in the cellar of his house in Hilldrop Crescent, Holloway, London.

All this because he was in love with his secretary, Ethel le Neve, who moved in with him after the murder. (He explained to friends that his wife had gone to America.) The police investigated but at first found nothing. Ethel, in the know but not a party to the murder, was still worried however - and rightly so as it turned out. The couple fled and, shortly after, the police discovered the remains of Crippen's wife in the cellar. Meanwhile the two lovers had boarded a liner bound for New York under the names Mr and Master Robinson. Unfortunately for them, the Captain had read a newspaper report about Hilldrop Crescent and became suspicious. He radioed to London and a detective was sent out in a fast ship to arrest the couple. Crippen was later hanged in Pentonville Prison.

Crompton, Samuel

Inventor who could spin a yarn

1753-1827

Samuel Crompton's mother was very strict. Every day after his school work she made him do some spinning or weaving as well. The family was short of money.

The spinning-jenny which he used for his spinning was always breaking down and it was this which drove him to invent a new machine. His invention became known as 'Crompton's Mule', because like a mule it was a cross-breed: it was a mixture of two earlier inventions. For secrecy, he worked on it at night and the neighbours thought his house was haunted because of all the late night banging and flashing lights. Due to lack of money he had to sell his invention for a mere £67, even though it could spin yarn which was finer than expensive Indian imports. Later Parliament gave him £5000 in thanks for his services to the country.

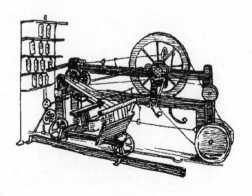

Cromwell, Oliver
"The Protector"

Ruler of England during the Commonwealth, when there was no king

1599-1658

Oliver Cromwell was a simple Cambridgeshire squire. In 1642, he formed a troop of cavalry (mounted soldiers) to fight against **Charles I** in the Civil War between Parliament and the King. Cromwell's 'Ironsides' became the spearhead of the Parliamentary Army.

He was leader of the 'Independents', who believed in religious toleration for everyone, including Roman Catholics* and Jews. Unfortunately they didn't believe in being tolerant to poor Charles I, who was beheaded in 1649. Cromwell was by then the strongest leader in parliament and became 'Lord Protector' of the Commonwealth which followed (1649-1660). He ruled England like a king - quite a good one too.

The monarchy was restored under **Charles II**, who pardoned his enemies - all except the 'regicides' who had signed the death warrant of his father. Cromwell's body was dug up and hung from a gallows, his head being stuck on a pole on top of Westminster Hall.

Cromwell, Thomas

Statesman who got rid of the monasteries - but couldn't keep his head

1485-1540

120 Thomas Cromwell was **Henry VIII's** adviser. It was probably Cromwell who suggested to Henry that he break with the Pope and start the Church of England and it was Cromwell who suggested that Henry 'dissolve' the English monasteries, sell their lands and take the money.

The son of a London blacksmith, in his youth Cromwell was a ruffian who had to flee England because of some crime, serving as a soldier in France and as a clerk in Antwerp. He rose to power on the coat-tails of Henry's 241 great chancellor **Cardinal Wolsey**, becoming his secretary. When Wolsey fell from Henry's favour in 1529, Cromwell had the courage to stand up for his old boss. Luckily for him, Henry respected this. Before long Cromwell was the most powerful of Henry's councillors, becoming Lord Great Chamberlain in 1539.

1539 was also the year of his undoing. He arranged Henry's marriage with the ugly Anne of Cleves - and paid the price. Accused of treason in June 1540, he was beheaded by the end of July. The axeman was clumsy and his death was 'unusually revolting'.

Darby, Abraham

Manufacturer of cast iron things

around 1677-1717

Abraham Darby was the son of a Midlands farmer, but he was always more interested in manufacturing than he was in farming. In 1704 he opened a brass factory in Bristol. He then had the idea that it might be possible to make pots and pans out of iron instead of brass. He experimented with various methods of casting iron and eventually hit on a brand new method using sand. Before long his strong, cheap pans were being sold all over Britain.

In 1709, he had moved back to the Midlands, to Coalbrookdale in Shropshire where he leased an old furnace. It was there that he first smelted iron using coke as the fuel. This was a far more reliable fuel than coal or charcoal, which were all anyone had thought of using up to then. Now good quality cast iron was plentifully available for the first time. Many things, including factory machinery, are made of iron. Abraham Darby's cast iron helped Britain to become the first country in the world to industrialise.

Darling, Grace Horsley

Lighthouse heroine

1815-42

On 7 September 1838 the waves grew wild around the storm-lashed Farne Islands off the coast of Northumberland. The regular Forfarshire steamboat was smashed up by the huge waves. Nine men and a woman survived by clinging to a lonely rock. Luckily for them a nearby lighthouse-keeper, William Darling by name, saw what had happened. He was alone in his lighthouse apart from his wife and his seventh daughter, Grace. He asked Grace to help him rescue the survivors. They rowed into the storm in a small boat and managed to carry four men and a woman back to the lighthouse. William and two of the rescued men then went back for the rest.

The British public loved it! Grace was the heroine of the hour. She and her father had to sit for seven portraits in eleven days. They were given money by the government. There were so many requests for locks of Grace's hair that she was said to be in danger of going bald. But Grace never let her fame go to her head. She lived quietly and happily on the island until her death from illness four years later. William lived on for another twenty-three years.

Darnley, Henry Stewart, Lord *see* Mary Queen of Scots

Darwin, Charles Robert

He put evolution on the map
1809-82

Charles Darwin was the son of a Shrewsbury doctor. In 1831 he joined a scientific expedition bound for South America and the Pacific Ocean on a sailing ship called *The Beagle* (1831-36). He was to be the ship's naturalist, the expert on plants and animals.

If ever there was a 'voyage of a lifetime', this was it. In the Galapagos Islands Darwin saw how the same species of birds, cut off for centuries on different islands, had developed in quite different ways. This and many other amazing discoveries led him to his theory of 'evolution by natural selection'. This theory lies behind all modern ideas on how different species of living things have come to be the way they are and how they will change in the future.

He didn't publish his ideas until 1858-9, long after he'd returned home. His book *The Origin of Species by Means of Natural Selection* raised a storm of protest among religious leaders because it seemed to deny the story of creation in the Bible. Darwin won the argument in the end - he's now buried in Westminster Abbey.

David I
"the Good King"

Saintly medieval monarch
- well, fairly saintly

around **1082-1153, KING OF SCOTLAND**

David's mother was a saint: Saint Margaret, the only royal saint in Scotland. So it's hardly surprising that he came to be called the 'Good King'.

At the age of thirteen, he was sent to the English court
114 with his two sisters. One sister, Matilda, married **Henry I**. Because of this, after David became king of Scotland in 1124, he backed Henry's daughter, also called
153 **Matilda** (the Empress Maud), in her struggle with King
208 **Stephen** for the English throne. David was finally defeated by Stephen at the Battle of the Standard in 1138. This battle is one of the main reasons that the northern counties of England are now a part of England and not of Scotland.

After 1138 David ruled peacefully and well. By the time he died, Scotland was a strong, independent country with its own laws.

Devereux, Robert *see* **Essex, Robert Devereux, Earl of**

Dickens, Charles

Very popular Victorian writer

1812-70

In 1821, all Charles Dickens' family except Charles were imprisoned for debt. At that time people could be sent to prison if they owed money. Left alone, eleven-year-old Charles had to work long hours in a factory just to pay for his rent and meals. On Sundays he visited his family.

After the factory he became a clerk, then a journalist where he learned how to write. Before long he was the most popular writer of his time. But the memory of those dark days never really left him. In later life, in books like *Oliver Twist* and *Bleak House*, he wrote about poverty or the struggles of poor children. His very name has become a word, 'Dickensian', used to describe scenes of nineteenth century gloom.

Fear of the debtors' prison never really left him. As well as writing he used to give public readings of his work. He kept touring Britain and America so as to earn as much money as possible. It may have been tiredness from too many performances which brought on his death in 1870.

Disraeli, Benjamin, Earl of Beaconsfield

"Dizzy"

Very Victorian Prime Minister

1804-81

Two Prime Ministers dominated the last half of Queen **Victoria's** long reign: **Gladstone**, the Liberal* - and Disraeli, the Tory*. They were like chalk and cheese. Victoria never liked Gladstone who was too serious. Dizzy was her favourite because he flattered her. It was due to Disraeli that she took the title 'Empress of India'. The son of a Jew but baptised a Christian at the age of thirteen, Disraeli was also a good writer. His first novel *Vivian Grey* was a big success.

223, 100

There's no room here for all the twists and turns of policy which he fought over during his long life. Enough to say that his 1867 Reform Bill gave many working class men the vote and in 1868 he became Prime Minister, starting his long duel for power with Gladstone. He was Prime Minister twice and ended up a very famous man indeed.

Dowding, Hugh Caswall Tremenheere, 1st Baron
" Stuffy "

Air chief who won the Battle of Britain

1882-1970

Without Hugh Dowding, it's very likely that Hitler's Germany would have invaded Britain in 1940. It was Dowding who organized Britain's air defences, and he did it brilliantly.

The younger officers gave him the nickname 'Stuffy' because he was old-fashioned and serious. But when in 1936 he was made Commander-in-Chief of 'Fighter Command', it turned out that Stuffy was just the man for the job. He planned ahead. Due to him, by the start of World War II in 1939, Britain had squadrons of the latest Spitfires and Hurricanes and a chain of brand new radar stations around the south and east coasts - where German air attacks would come from. The Battle of Britain was fought out over the skies of southern Britain during August and September 1940 with Dowding in control of the British planes. He was a brilliant commander, carefully looking after his hard-stretched men and machines. And because the Germans failed to win control of the skies over Britain, they were never able to risk landing their army on British shores.

Dowding lived on for many years after the war was over, honoured by his country.

Drake, Sir Francis

Tough Tudor sea dog who sailed round the world

around 1540-1596

Francis Drake was born in Devon at a time when many of England's best sailors came from that area. During his life Protestant* England was often at war with Catholic* Spain and there were rich pickings to be had by capturing Spanish ships. Drake, who was an incredibly bold and brilliant sailor, captured more than his fair share. He was also the first Englishman to sail round the world, which he did (1577-88) in his ship *The Golden Hind*, taking so much treasure from the Spanish that when he returned home his ship was weighed down with it.

85 In 1587, **Elizabeth I** put him in command of an expedition to attack a Spanish fleet which was getting ready to attack England. Drake sailed right into Cadiz harbour and wrecked the ships there, before going on to capture another hundred Spanish ships elsewhere. It was said that he'd 'singed the king of Spain's beard'. By 1588, he was Vice-Admiral of the fleet which defeated the Spanish Armada.

The Spanish called Drake a pirate but they were terrified of him. No doubt they were very pleased when he died on yet another mission to America the following year.

Dryden, John
" Poet Squab"

Poet with an eye for trouble

1631-1700

John Dryden was short, stout and red-faced. He was ugly (which was probably why he got the nickname 'Squab') but he wrote like an angel - or a demon. He was the most famous writer of his time, famous as much for wild comedies and savage poems as for more gentle poems. His brilliant pen sometimes got him into trouble. In one essay he attacked his fellow poet, John Wilmot, Earl of Rochester. Rochester was overheard to say that he would 'leave the repartee to Black Will with a cudgel'. Dryden was badly beaten up shortly after!

The son of a Northamptonshire rector, Dryden moved to London in 1650, living the life of a London 'wit'. He could be found almost any day of the year in one or other of London's many coffee houses. In May 1700, he had a bad attack of gout but refused to let his toe be cut off. He died shortly after and was buried beside 51 **Chaucer** in Westminster Abbey.

Duncan I   *see* **Macbeth**

Duncan II

died 1094, KING OF SCOTLAND

Duncan was killed by his unruly subjects after a short reign, having won the Scottish throne with the help of English and Norman knights lent by Robert, eldest son of **William the Conqueror**.

235

Edgar the Ætheling

Saxon prince who never became king

around 1050-1125

74 Edgar was a Saxon prince, the grandson of **Edmund Ironside**. He should have become king on the death of
74 his great-uncle **Edward the Confessor**, but he never
109 made it, his place being taken first by **Harold**
235 **Godwinsson** then by **William the Conqueror**. He made peace with William in 1074 and led armies for him in Scotland and Italy.

Edmund II
"Ironside"

Short-lived king who fought the vikings

around 1993-1016, SAXON KING OF ENGLAND

6
74

55

Edmund was the son of **Æthelred the Unready** and half-brother of **Edward the Confessor**. He was chosen to be king by the citizens of London in 1016 on the death of his father and fought brilliantly against **Cnut's** invading Viking army, earning his nickname 'Ironside'. Unfortunately, he was either murdered or died of sickness a few months later.

Edward
"the Confessor"

King who left a mess behind him

around 1003-66, SAXON KING OF ENGLAND

Edward was probably an albino, that is he had no dark colouring at all and his hair and beard were completely white, as was his skin. Although he was almost the last 'English' king of England before the Norman conquest of 1066, he was in fact more Norman than English, having been brought up in Normandy from the age of ten, almost until he became King in 1042. His reign was spoiled by quarrels between his Norman favourites and English nobles led by the powerful Earl Godwin of Wessex and his son **Harold Godwinsson**.

109

Edward was very religious. He built Westminster Abbey among other places. Legend said that he worked miracles and healed people and he was made a 'saint' in 1161. In reality however, although he was white as the driven snow he was no saint. Far from it: he left England in a mess when he died and opened the door to the Norman conquest.

Edward I
"Hammer of the Scots"

Good English king - but not so good for the Scots

1239-1307, KING OF ENGLAND (PLANTAGENET)

116

Edward I , eldest son of **Henry III**, was a fighter, and a very good one. Once while on crusade in Palestine, he was attacked by a member of the secret sect of the Assassins while in his bed. Edward wrestled the knife from the Assassin, kicked him to the ground and stabbed him with his own weapon. On another occasion a kick from a horse broke two of his ribs just

224

before battle with the Scottish leader **William Wallace**, but Edward mounted and rode on as if nothing had happened. He won the battle.

On marriage to his beloved wife Eleanor of Castile, he

was given Gascony, Ireland, Wales, Bristol, Stamford and Grantham by his father - some wedding present! But he still had to fight for them, putting down a rebellion in Wales and conquering Scotland (which he hadn't been given but got anyway). Wales stayed part of his kingdom, ringed by a necklace of massive, new English castles, but after he died in 1307 the Scots under 30 **Robert the Bruce** regained their independence.

Edward II

Measly medieval monarch

1284-1327, KING OF ENGLAND (PLANTAGENET)

Edward II was groomed for greatness by his powerful 75 father, **Edward I**. When only six, he was engaged to be married to the infant Queen Margaret of Scotland and if she hadn't died Scotland and England would have been united more than 300 years earlier than actually happened. In 1301 he was made the very first Prince of Wales by his father.

But all that grooming couldn't change his weak character. He gambled, drank and spent money like water. In 1307 he went to France to marry Isabella, daughter of the French king, leaving his favourite, Piers de Gaveston, in charge of the kingdom. The English nobles loathed Gaveston (and Edward too). They killed Gaveston while Edward was out of the country.

Worse was to follow: in 1325 Isabella, who despised her royal husband, visited the French court and promptly 166 fell in love with a nobleman, **Roger de Mortimer**. Next year she invaded England. No one came to Edward's defence. He was captured and brutally murdered on the orders of his wife and her lover.

Edward III
" the King of the Sea"

Warrior king who died alone
1312-77, KING OF ENGLAND (PLANTAGENET)

76 Edward III, the son of **Edward II**, was a warrior king, coming to the throne in 1325 at the age of fifteen shortly before his father was murdered.

The Hundred Years' War between England and France began during his reign (1337-1453). This suited Edward because he loved fighting even more than he loved hunting or feasting. In 1344, he founded the Order of the Garter for his noble warrior companions. He spent money like water, wore the very best clothes and was brave as a lion, once even fighting as an ordinary knight so as to get close to the enemy. His most crushing victories against the French were the sea Battle of Sluys (1340) and the Battle of Crecy (1346). The great victory of Poitiers (1349) was won by his son the Black Prince.

In 1348 the Plague struck England for the first time and by 1357 half the population had died. Edward may have been dashing, but he never cared much for the suffering of common people. He himself died unloved and almost alone twenty years later. His mistress, Alice Perrers, stole the rings from his dead fingers.

Edward IV

Handsome king in troubled times

1442-83, KING OF ENGLAND (HOUSE OF YORK)

Edward IV was King of England from 1461 during the Wars of the Roses* (1455-85), a struggle for power between the families of Lancaster and York. Edward's emblem was the red rose of York. He was handsome and popular and is generally thought to have been a good king in troubled times. He came to throne at the young age of nineteen and died at the (relatively) young age of forty.

Edward V

Prince in the Tower

1470-83, KING OF ENGLAND (HOUSE OF YORK)

Edward V was the eldest son of **Edward IV**. He became King of England when only twelve on the death of his father. A few months later he too was dead - he and his younger brother were the two 'princes in the tower' who were probably murdered in the Tower of London on the orders of their uncle, Richard Duke of Gloucester 196 (soon to be **Richard III**). The two princes may have been suffocated by having pillows pressed over their faces.

Edward VI

Young Protestant who popped off early

1537-53, KING OF ENGLAND (TUDOR)

Edward was a bookish boy. He preferred studying to sport on the whole and was a very clever student. As 120 **Henry VIII's** only son, he became king on the death of his father (1547) even though he had two elder sisters, 150, **Mary** and **Elizabeth**. He was only ten years old so the 85 kingdom was governed by his uncle, Edward Seymour, Duke of Somerset and 'Lord Protector' - until Seymour was executed a few years later by rivals for power.

Edward was a Protestant* and it was during his reign that the Church of England became a truly Protestant church and the beautiful *Book of Common Prayer* was 59 produced by **Thomas Cranmer**. But his health was never strong. In January 1553 he became ill after catching cold in a tennis match and was dead by July - it was sport, not books, which killed him.

Edward VII

1841-1910, KING OF GREAT BRITAIN AND IRELAND

Edward, known as Bertie to his friends, was the eldest son of **Queen Victoria**, but she reigned so long that he didn't become king till 1901 when he was sixty. 'Bertie' loved horse racing, sailing, the theatre and women.

223

Edward VIII

1894-1972, KING OF GREAT BRITAIN AND IRELAND

99 Edward was the eldest son of **George V**. He was forced to abdicate (give up the crown) in 1936, the year of his coronation, because he wanted to marry Mrs Wallis Simpson, a divorced American. Divorce was very frowned on in those days.

Edwin

He started Northumbria

around **584-632, KING OF NORTHUMBRIA**

Edwin lived at a time when Saxon England was divided into several small kingdoms. As a child he was heir to

Deira in the north-east but was forced to live in exile by the King of Bernicia even further to the north. In 617 he fought his way to the throne of Deira then conquered Bernicia as well. His newly combined kingdom of Northumbria was one of the mightiest Saxon kingdoms.

In 625 he married Æthelburgh, the Christian daughter of the King of Kent, and became a Christian. He ruled wisely and well. It was said that during his reign a woman and child could walk from one end of Northumbria to the other without coming to any harm.

183 Not for long however. In 632 **Penda**, the King of Mercia in the Midlands, and Caedwalla, a Welsh king who hated Saxons, killed Edwin after a ferocious battle and slaughtered hundreds of his subjects. Edwin was forty-eight - not bad for a Saxon king.

Egbert

He got the lot - and lost it

died 839, SAXON KING OF ENGLAND

Egbert is known as the first ruler of all Saxon England. In 802 he became King of Wessex, the land of the West Saxons. Then in 829, he conquered Mercia (in the Midlands). He was then recognized as over-king by the northern Saxon kingdom of Northumbria. A year later, however, he lost Mercia and the last few years of his life were spent fighting Viking raiders and other enemies.

Eleanor of Aquitaine

Medieval lady with lots of land

around 1122-1204, QUEEN OF ENGLAND

Eleanor was the daughter of the Duke of Aquitaine, which is a huge chunk of territory in the centre and south of France. In 1152 she married Henry Plantagenet, Count of Anjou, another huge chunk of France. Then in 1154 Henry became King **Henry II** of England, and became Duke of Normandy (*another* huge chunk of France) two years later. Partly due to Eleanor, the English crown now controlled over half of France.

Eleanor helped her sons, the future kings **Richard I** and **John,** in a rebellion against their father and spent sixteen years as a prisoner for it. When Richard became King she stood in for him while he was away fighting in the crusades*.

Elgar, Sir Edward William

Enigmatic English composer

1857-1934

Elgar is one of the most famous British composers. He had a good start, being the son of a Worcester organist, but mainly he taught himself. Among his best known works are *The Dream of Gerontius*, *The Enigma Variations* and his cello concerto. He became 'Master of the King's Music' in 1924 at the height of his fame. He came from Malvern in Worcestershire, where he spent most of his life.

Eliot, George

Nice books - clever woman

1819-80

George Eliot's real name for most of her life was Mary Ann (or Marian) Evans. George Eliot was just the 'pen name' she used on her books. Since she was one of the greatest English novelists of the nineteenth century the pen name has stuck. Her greatest novels are: *Adam Bede*, *The Mill on the Floss*, *Silas Marner* and *Middlemarch*.

In 1854, she fell in love with a writer called George Henry Lewes (where the 'George' in George Eliot came from). They were two of the ugliest people in London. Ugly on the outside - but clever and kind on the inside. It was Lewes who encouraged her to start writing novels. Just one cloud cast its shadow: Lewes was separated from his wife, but divorce was almost impossible in those days so he couldn't marry Mary Ann. They had to live together unmarried.

After Lewes died in 1878, Mary Ann finally did get married - to a banker who was twenty years younger than her. But Lewes was the love of her life. When Mary Ann died, she was buried next to him.

Eliot, TS
(Thomas Stearns)

Modern poet who came to stay

1888-1965

TS Eliot started life as an American. His first major poem, *The Lovesong of J Alfred Prufrock*, was written in America. He qualifies for this book because he left America when he was twenty-two, settled in England and became an Englishman.

His poems used everyday speech in a new way. *The Waste Land*, published in 1922 in both Britain and America, started a revolution in how modern poetry is written. By this time Eliot had lived in England for six years and was already turning into an Englishman. The change was complete by 1927 when he became a British citizen and a member of the Church of England. His greatest poems, 'The Four Quartets', are very English in a quiet sort of way. They are: *Burnt Norton*, *East Coker*, *The Dry Salvages* and *Little Gidding*.

East Coker was the Somerset village from which Eliot's ancestors had left for America many years before - it was in East Coker church that his ashes were buried in 1965.

Elizabeth I
" the Virgin Queen "

T op queen who married her country

1533-1603, QUEEN OF ENGLAND AND IRELAND (TUDOR)

In 1536 when she was only two, Elizabeth's father **Henry VIII** murdered her mother, **Anne Boleyn** so that he could marry someone else - well, he had her executed anyway. No wonder Elizabeth never married.

120, 24

She was brought up in dangerous times. As a Protestant* she was in greatest danger once her fiercely

150 Catholic* sister **Mary** became Queen in 1553. In fact she ended up in the Tower of London and nearly had her head chopped off like her mother.

Nearly but not quite. In 1558, Mary's short reign came to an end and Elizabeth became Queen. She reigned for forty-five years and was perhaps the greatest ruler of England ever, steering her mainly Protestant country through all kinds of plots which would have caused huge bloodshed if they'd succeeded. Along the way, 151 she executed Catholic **Mary Queen of Scots** for plotting against her and defeated an invasion force known as the Spanish Armada (1588), although she herself was never bloodthirsty - by the standards of her time.

'Elizabethan' England is still thought of as a golden age: 198, 190, the age of **Shakespeare**, **Walter Raleigh** and **Francis** 71 **Drake** among many others. As the 'Virgin Queen' she reigned over a whole galaxy of brilliant Elizabethans. Undoubtedly there were some among them, such as 88 Robert Dudley and **Robert Devereux**, whom she loved during her long life, but in the end she settled for the love of her subjects. Which they gave her - most of the time anyway.

Elizabeth of York

Nice girl with golden hair who married Henry VII

1465-1503, QUEEN OF ENGLAND

Elizabeth was beautiful and gentle. She had long golden hair. She was the eldest daughter of the King **Edward IV** and she was born during the Wars of the Roses* (1455-85) fought between the families of York and Lancaster. Her father was a Yorkist as was she. In 1485, her future husband Henry Tudor won the Battle of Bosworth, last battle of the Wars of the Roses, and became **Henry VII**. Henry was on the side of Lancaster, but he was no fool: five months later he married Elizabeth and thus united both York and Lancaster into one family - and ended the Wars of the Roses for good.

Essex, Robert Devereux, Earl of

Long-legged Tudor favourite who fell out with Elizabeth I

1566-1601

Robert Devereux charged through life like a whirlwind. He used to shovel down breakfast then throw on whatever clothes came to hand. He was very tall and prowled the court of **Elizabeth I** 'like the neck of a giraffe'. From 1587 he rose to be Elizabeth's favourite. They used to play cards together until deep into the night.

Robert was charming - but he was in too much of a hurry and although a brave soldier he was a poor general. In 1599, he begged to be allowed to lead an expedition against Irish rebels. It was a failure. Desperate to keep Elizabeth's favour, he left his army and rushed back to London. He burst into her bedchamber all spattered in mud from his wild gallop across England. She had her wig off at the time and she wasn't amused.

First he was ordered away from court, then he was imprisoned in his London mansion. After a mad and desperate attempt to seize power by force, he was executed. It took three blows of the executioner's axe to chop off his head.

Faraday, Michael

Scientist who invented the electric motor

1791-1867

Michael Faraday was the son of a blacksmith. He taught himself science, but not maths, while working for a bookbinder. He's probably the only great scientist to have been useless at maths.

In 1812 he became assistant to Humphrey Davy, a leading scientist at the Royal Institute. Davy's wife treated young Faraday like a servant but he tried to ignore her rudeness and worked hard in Davy's laboratory. He was far too clever to remain an assistant for long. By 1824, he'd been elected to the Royal Society* and the discoveries were flowing thick and fast. The chemical benzine and the laws of electrolysis were just for starters: above all, it was Faraday who invented the first electric motor and the first electric generator and discovered the scientific laws which govern them.

Today we take electricity for granted. Without Faraday's discoveries we wouldn't be able to.

Fawkes, Guy

Good guy - bad plotter

1570-1606

Guy Fawkes (well - a model of him called a 'guy') is burned on thousands of bonfires every 5 November. He's burned to celebrate the fact that he failed to blow up **James I** and Parliament on 5 November 1605.

In 1604 James I, a Protestant*, was worried about Catholic* plans to seize his kingdom and force it to turn Catholic. Tough new laws were passed against English Catholics. The 'Gunpowder Plot' to blow up Parliament was hatched soon afterwards by a group of desperate young Catholics by way of a reply. Guy was the son of English Protestants but he'd turned Catholic when quite young and had fought in the Catholic Spanish army. He was the explosives expert of the plot. The plotters rented a cellar which ran beneath the House of Lords and he was put in charge of packing it full of barrels of gunpowder. On 4 November he was caught red-handed in the cellar after the plot had been given away. He was cool and brave under torture, but it made no difference to his final punishment. He and his fellow plotters were tried and executed five days later.

Fleming, Alexander

Scientist who discovered penicillin

1881-1955

Alexander Fleming was the son of a Scottish sheep farmer. Through luck and hard work he became a surgeon at St Mary's Hospital, Paddington in 1908.

In 1928 he was at St Mary's, working on research into bacteria which cause many diseases. One day he noticed that a dish of bacteria which he'd left uncovered for a few days had gone mouldy. This was nothing in itself, but Fleming also noticed that the bacteria around each speck of mould had died: the mould must be producing a bacteria-killer. The mould was *'penicillium notatum'*, a close relation to the mould that grows on stale bread, so he called the bacteria-killer 'penicillin'. Further research showed that it was harmless to animals and people, which was important because it meant that it could be used as a medicine - the first antibiotic. He was not a chemist and it took two other scientists, Florey and Chain, to find ways of producing it in quantity in the 1940s. Florey, Chain and Fleming shared the Nobel prize for medicine in 1945.

Frobisher, Sir Martin

Terribly tough Tudor sea dog

around 1535-1594

Martin Frobisher was tough - very tough. He was arrested several times for piracy. He was also strong: he once lifted an Inuit, canoe and all, into his ship. (The Inuit was so angry he bit his own tongue in two.)

Between 1576 and 1578 Frobisher made three voyages in search of a north-west passage around the north coast of America to China and, more to the point, in search of gold which he thought he'd found in Frobisher Bay. He brought back 200 tons of black ore, but it turned out to be worthless. He never found the north-west passage either, but he did explore far along the northern coasts of America and was the first modern European explorer to enter the Arctic circle in that region.

In 1588 he was knighted for his bravery while fighting against the Spanish invasion fleet, the Armada. After further adventures, mainly in search of Spanish treasure ships, he died from a battle wound taken on the French coast.

Fry, Elizabeth

Prison reformer who cooked up a change

1780-1845

Elizabeth Fry was one of the Fry family who invented Fry's Chocolate Creams. More importantly, in 1813 she visited Newgate Prison for women and found a hell on earth: three hundred women lived in two wards and two cells with their children. They slept on the bare floor and there were no bedclothes. The prisoners fought, gambled, danced and swore.

Elizabeth set out to put things right. She gathered clothes for the poorest prisoners, she started a school inside the prison, she arranged for a matron to be in charge. And she preached to them: Elizabeth was a Quaker* and her words could make the hardest criminals weep and feel sorry for their crimes.

The rest of her life was spent in trying to improve prison conditions and in starting hostels for the homeless. She became famous throughout Europe but was always a true Quaker who kept faith with the poor.

Gainsborough, Thomas

Artist who made a splash in society

1727-88

Thomas Gainsborough was the youngest of nine children. They were a clever family: one brother made himself wings and tried to fly, another experimented with steam engines. Gainsborough was cleverest of the lot. He grew up to be one of the greatest English landscape and portrait painters.

When still a boy he loved to sketch the country around Sudbury, the Suffolk town where they lived. It was the same sort of flat eastern landscape later beloved by another great painter, **John Constable**. Later, fame and fortune drew him away to fashionable Bath and London where his portraits were prized by the highest in the land.

57

If you had to change lives with someone, Gainsborough's wouldn't be a bad life to choose. He married young and happily (when he and his wife quarrelled they used to make up by sending notes to each other signed with the names of their dogs - which the dogs carried), he had good friends and he died rich and famous.

George I

German who preferred Germany

1660-1727, KING OF GREAT BRITAIN AND IRELAND (HOUSE OF HANOVER)

George I was the first Hanoverian King of Great Britain. His claim to the throne was that he was the great grandson of **James I** - and he was a Protestant*. He was also German. When summoned to be king in 1714, he was the fifty-four-year-old 'Elector' of Hanover, a small state in the middle of Germany - which is why he's called 'Hanoverian'.

Like most Hanoverians, George was a hopeless family man. He and his wife loathed each other. He also loathed his son, the future **George II** (who loathed him back). He never learned English and preferred Germany to England. He died in Holland while on his way to Hanover with a mistress, the (German) Duchess of Kendal. During his reign Britain was dominated by the Prime Minister **Robert Walpole**.

George II
"the Little Captain"

A German - but not so German as his father

1683-1760, KING OF GREAT BRITAIN AND IRELAND (HOUSE OF HANOVER)

George was thirty-one in 1714 when he moved to England from Germany with his father, **George I**. He never lost his strong German accent, but he still liked to taunt his father's German courtiers by saying that the English were nicer and better looking than they were. He became King in 1727 when George I died.

As with most of the Georges, family matters weren't his strong point. He loathed his father and fell out with his eldest son, Frederick Prince of Wales (died 1751). He did however love his wife, Queen Caroline - after a fashion: she just had to put up with his mistresses. During his thirty-three year reign, the country was dominated by the Prime Ministers **Robert Walpole** and later, **William Pitt the Elder**.

George III
"Farmer George"

Long-lived king who gained one empire and lost another

1738-1820, KING OF GREAT BRITAIN AND IRELAND (HOUSE OF HANOVER)

96 George III, grandson of **George II**, reigned for sixty years. Sixty years during which Britain won one huge empire in India and Canada and lost another one - the future USA. George would have liked to keep America. During his reign the country was dominated by two 50 brilliant Prime Ministers: **William Pitt the Elder** and 186 later by Pitt's son, **William Pitt the Younger**.

Like all the Georges, George III loathed his eldest son, 98 the future **George IV**. He was however the only George to have a truly happy marriage. He lived simply with his wife Queen Charlotte at Kew, where he farmed and gardened. He went mad in his later years and is said to have died from trying too hard on the toilet.

George IV
" Prinny "

Fast-living prince of the 'Regency Period'

**1762-1830, KING OF GREAT BRITAIN AND IRELAND
(HOUSE OF HANOVER)**

97   By 1811 **George III** had gone seriously mad. His son, the future George IV, was made 'Prince Regent' and reigned in his place. Nine years later George III died and George IV was at last crowned. He's famous for building the Brighton Pavilion and for the Regency Period of beautiful clothes and fast-living Regency 'bucks', as the fashionable young men of the time were called.

Like all the Georges he had family problems. In 1785 he secretly married a Mrs Fitzherbert. He was too young to marry without permission and anyway she was a Catholic*, so the marriage didn't count. Ten years later he married Princess Caroline of Brunswick; they loathed each other from the start. He also fell out with his daughter. In later life he became horribly fat.

George V

1865-1936, King of Great Britain and Ireland
(House of Windsor)

80 George was only the second son of his father **Edward VII** and never expected to become king. Then when he was twenty-six his elder brother, Prince Eddy, died and George found himself heir to the throne. He stayed popular from his coronation in 1910 until his death twenty-six years later.

George VI

1895-1952, King of Great Britain and Ireland
(House of Windsor)

George VI was the second son of **George V**. He became
80 king when his elder brother **Edward VIII** abdicated in 1936. He was a popular figurehead for the people of Britain during the darkest days of World War II.

Gladstone, William Ewart

Very Victorian Prime Minister

1809-98

Two great politicians dominated Britain during the last half of Queen **Victoria's** reign: one was **Disraeli**, a Tory*, the other was Gladstone, a Liberal*. Victoria liked Disraeli and couldn't stand Gladstone. She felt that he preached at her during their meetings.

223, 69

Gladstone first became an MP in 1832 and finally resigned from Parliament in 1894. During those sixty-two years he was Prime Minister of four governments and Leader of the Opposition for much of the rest of the time. He'd actually started off as a Tory but had soon become a Liberal, which meant among other things that he wanted working class men to have the vote and he later supported 'Home Rule' for Ireland. He died as he lived - seriously, spending the last few weeks in prayer.

Glendower, Owen

Welsh rebel who wouldn't give up

around 1359-1416

In 1401 Owen Glendower, a wealthy Welsh lord, attacked his English neighbour, Lord Grey, in a quarrel over some land. At that time many of the Welsh were angry with King **Henry IV** of England. They had preferred **Richard II** whom Henry had murdered a year before. Owen's attack sparked off a general Welsh rebellion. In the war that followed, the English tended to control the towns and castles but the Welsh could vanish into their hills - the English soldiers said that Glendower had the power to make himself invisible.

116
195

By 1404 he controlled most of Wales. Calling himself 'Prince of Wales', he started an independent Welsh parliament and ruled like a king. But England was far too powerful. By 1411 after another seven years of fighting, Henry IV felt strong enough to issue a pardon to all the rebels except Glendower and one other. In 1413 the old man himself was pardoned - except that he fought on. Glendower may have died of starvation in the Welsh mountains.

Glyndwr Owain *see above* **Glendower**

Godwin, Earl *see* **Harold II**

Gordon, Charles George
"Chinese Gordon"

Victorian soldier who died at Khartoum

1833-85

Gordon was a very Victorian soldier. He was brave, stern and honest. In 1860 he was in China as part of a French/British force which captured Peking. He commanded the senseless destruction of the Chinese Emperor's beautiful summer palace and later helped put down the Taiping Rebellion.

In 1877 he was made Governor of Sudan by the Khedive of Egypt who then ruled Sudan. He worked flat out, suppressing the slave trade among other things, but had to retire due to bad health. But by 1884, Sudan had been overrun by rebels led by a brilliant leader known as 'the Mahdi', and the Khedive asked Gordon to help out once more. Gordon advanced into Sudan but was besieged in Khartoum from March 1884 until January 1885, when the Mahdi's rebels finally smashed his tiny band of defenders and killed Gordon on the steps of the palace. Two days later a relief force from Egypt arrived. As well as being called 'Chinese Gordon', Gordon was now 'Gordon of Khartoum' and a national hero in Britain.

Grace, WG
(William Gilbert)

Cricketing hero

1848-1915

William Grace, 'WG' as he was known, was the first great modern cricketer. During his very long career in first class cricket (1864-1908) he made 100 centuries, scored 54,896 runs and took 2,876 wickets. He was a large, burly man with a big dark beard.

He was a brilliant all-round athlete. He once slipped away from fielding at the Oval, rushed across London to the 1867 meeting of the National Olympian Association at Crystal Palace, won the hurdles, then returned to the Oval and scored a century!

Grey, Lady Jane
also called Lady Jane Dudley

Nine-days Queen

1537-54

Lady Jane was beautiful and clever. She was only seventeen when her head was chopped off on the orders of her cousin, Queen **Mary**. Mary was a Catholic* and Jane was a Protestant*.

Her problem was that she had royal blood in her veins: she was the cousin of King **Edward VI**. That's why her father forced her to marry a nobleman called Guilford Dudley, so that, through her, his friends the Dudleys could become the next royal family of England. (Edward VI was sickly and had no children to inherit his crown.) Jane hated the Dudleys from the moment she was forced to marry their son. They used to pinch and hurt her, in fact they cared *nothing* for her and *everything* for the crown of England.

Edward died on 6 July 1553. Jane fainted when the Dudleys told her that she was to be Queen. But she needn't have bothered fainting - she ruled for just nine days. Mary Tudor, Edward VI's elder sister, took power and became Queen Mary. She soon arrested her young rival on a charge of high treason. On 12 February 1554, on a green hill outside the Tower of London, Jane was forced to watch as her husband's bleeding, headless body slumped to the ground, and then she too was beheaded.

Gwyn, Nell *see* **Charles II**

Haig, Douglas

World War I general

1861-1928

Field Marshal Douglas Haig was Commander-in-Chief of British forces in Europe during most of World War I. He accepted horrific losses among his own men in the hope of breaking through German lines in the west. ¹⁴⁵ **David Lloyd George**, War Minister and later Prime Minister, disagreed with him, distrusted him and felt that there must be another way to win the war - but couldn't think of one.

In 1916, Haig launched the Somme offensive together with the French. 420,000 British soldiers died; Haig was promoted to Field Marshal. Next year, with the French on the defensive, he ordered a purely British attack. The Battle of Ypres was a massacre for the British, but it did at least weaken the Germans and helped lead to their defeat a year later. Haig was made Earl Haig of Bermersyde in 1919 by a 'grateful nation'.

Handel, George Frederick

Composer who wrote *The Messiah*

1685-1759

In 1710 Handel became a musician at the court of George, the Elector of Hanover, in Germany. He soon fell out of favour with the Elector due to spending too much time in London, where his operas were popular. Then in 1714 the Elector was crowned King **George I** of Britain and moved to - London! Handel had a problem.

He solved it by writing *Water Music*, played on a barge which followed the King's barge on the Thames one summer's day in 1715. George loved it and Handel was back in favour. Before long he was living full time in England. (He became a British citizen in 1726.) His greatest works are 'oratorios' sung in the English language and the greatest of these is *The Messiah*. It was first performed in Dublin in April 1742. In order to fit the audience of 700 into the hall, ladies were asked to come without the hoops which held out their dresses and gentlemen were asked to come without their swords.

The Messiah is still sung by hundreds of British choirs every year.

Hardeknut

He lived hard and died young

around 1018-1042, DANISH KING OF ENGLAND

Hardeknut was a typical Viking - he died of 'convulsions' brought on by too much drink. He was the son and heir of **Cnut**, but was in Denmark and unable to claim the throne of England when Cnut died in 1035. His rival and half-brother **Harold Harefoot** was elected over-king in his absence. Harefoot died in 1040 just before Hardeknut got to England to demand his crown. Hardeknut's death came two years later.

55

108

Hardie, James Keir

Scottish socialist* who helped start the Labour Party

1856-1915

Keir Hardie grew up in Scotland in terrible poverty. By the age of ten he was working down a coal mine. The only school he ever went to was evening school. Despite this poor start, he became a journalist, a trades union organizer for the Scottish miners and then an MP (first time 1892).

An early leader of the Labour Party and founder of the Independent Labour Party (1893), he was loved by his followers and hated by his opponents. A pacifist, he was against fighting in wars and in 1900 lost an election to Parliament due to speaking against the Boer War. Pacifism may well have led to his death: he was bitterly upset when the Labour Party decided to support Britain's effort in World War I. He withdrew from politics and by August 1914 he had caught pneumonia (a common disease among miners). He died the following year.

Harold Harefoot

died 1040, DANISH KING OF ENGLAND

55 Harold was the younger son of **Cnut**. He was elected over-king of England in 1037 but took ill and died three years later. He was buried at Westminster but his body 107 was dug up by his half-brother and rival, **Hardeknut**, and probably thrown in the Thames. It was later rescued and reburied elsewhere.

Harold II
(Godwinsson)

Saxon king who lost his country to the Normans

around 1020-1066, SAXON KING OF ENGLAND

Harold II was the last Saxon King of England. He was chosen King in January 1066 on the death of **Edward the Confessor**. By October he was dead.

74

In September 1066, Harold's brother Tostig and the ferocious Viking leader, Harald Hardrada, invaded the north of the country. Harold II defeated them at the Battle of Stamford Bridge on 25 September. He had no time to enjoy his victory however: just four days later **William the Conqueror** landed in the south. William was also after Harold's crown.

235

Harold and his army raced south. They met William's Norman army at Hastings on the Sussex coast on 14 October. Harold's Saxons fought all day but by dusk their shield wall was unbroken. Then William ordered his archers to shoot into the air so that their arrows fell within the shield wall. Harold is said to have been killed by an arrow in the eye. Saxon England died with him.

Harvey, William

Doctor who discovered the circulation of the blood

1578-1657

In his middle years, William Harvey was called 'The Circulator' because he discovered the circulation of the blood. *Circulator* was Latin slang for a quack (a false doctor). Not everyone liked the idea of blood circulating, which was why they called him names.

Since the time of the famous Greek doctor Galen (around 130-201) most doctors had been telling their patients that blood swishes back and forth in the veins and arteries. Harvey proved that blood flows round and round. He showed that it flows from the heart to the arteries then back up the veins to the lungs and heart in one direction only - that it circulates. He published his theory in a small book called *On the Motion of the Heart and Blood* (originally in Latin) in 1628.

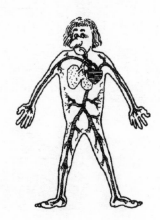

Hastings, Warren

Administrator of Bengal who got in a fight

1732-1818

In 1772 Warren Hastings became Governor General of Bengal, the first big Indian province to be ruled by the British. At that time the government of Bengal was riddled with corruption and its tax and legal systems were a mess. Hastings set out to put things right. A scholar, he respected Indian culture and believed that Indian traditions should be left alone - but he also thought that the British should run things, since they were in power, and it was therefore up to them to put things right.

Noses were put out of joint - both Indian noses and British noses. Indians lost power and the British feared they would lose money. Unfortunately Hastings had to rule with four other members of a 'Supreme Council' most of whom were against him. In 1780, he fought a duel with his main opponent and wounded him.

In 1788, his enemies forced him to stand trial in the House of Lords. The trial went on for seven long years before he was acquitted.

Hawkins, Sir John

Tough Tudor sea dog

1532-95

Sir John Hawkins was born in Plymouth where many Elizabethan sailors came from. He was a typical sailor of his time: tough as old leather, very greedy, probably dishonest - and a brilliant sea captain.

In 1562, he became the first Englishman to take part in the slave trade, until then run by the Spanish and Portuguese. He captured or bought Africans on the west coast of Africa and sold them as slaves in the Spanish West Indies. The Spanish weren't allowed to trade with most foreigners, but they had to in his case - at the point of a gun.

In 1577, he became treasurer of the English navy. Due to him, new, faster ships were built. Hawkins' new ships helped defeat the great Spanish Armada when it sailed up the English Channel in 1588. He died at sea, during an expedition to the West Indies.

Hengist

First Saxon King in England

died around 488

Hengist and Horsa were two Saxon brothers who led the first Saxon invasion of Britain. There had been many Saxon hit and run attacks before, but theirs was different. Invited to Britain by **Vortigern**, a British ruler, to help him fight the Picts and Scots, they landed in Kent in three or more open boats around 449. Six years later they turned on Vortigern, defeating him in a battle in which Horsa was killed. Then in 457 the Saxon warriors under Hengist slaughtered 4,000 Britons at the Battle of Crecgan Ford. Hengist was now a king, the very first Saxon king in England. Both their names probably mean 'horse' - which seems pretty obvious in the case of Horsa.

224

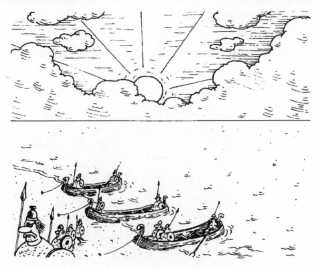

Henry I
"Beauclerc"
(meaning 'Good Scholar')

Norman who married a Saxon

1069-1135, KING OF ENGLAND (NORMAN)

235 Henry I was the youngest son of **William the Conqueror** and the only one to be born in England rather than Normandy. Crowned in 1100 on the death
237 of his middle brother **William II**, he was the first Norman king to bring together his Norman and Saxon subjects so that they started to think of themselves as one English people. One way he did this was by marrying Eadgyth (Mathilda), a Scottish princess who was descended from the old Saxon royal family. Others followed his example and mixed marriages became much more common.

In later life Henry grew fat. He died of a fever brought on by eating a 'surfeit of lampreys' (a primitive kind of fish, which he ate too much of).

Henry II

Good king with family problems

1133-89, KING OF ENGLAND (PLANTAGENET)

114 Henry II, grandson of **Henry I**, never sat down from morning to night, wore any old clothes and cared nothing for comfort - his own or other people's. He was one of the great medieval kings of England, ruling for thirty-four years from 1154.

20 In 1162 he fell out with his friend **Thomas à Becket**, then Archbishop of Canterbury. Thomas was murdered, perhaps on Henry's orders, and Henry had to do 'penance' by being beaten by each of the seventy monks of Canterbury Cathedral. Even worse than this were
82 quarrels with his four sons by his wife **Eleanor of Aquitaine**. In 1173 Eleanor, Henry (junior), Geoffrey
194 and Richard, the future **Richard I**, all rebelled against Henry I. He crushed the rebellion, but family troubles didn't stop. In 1189, Richard rebelled again, forcing Henry to name him as his heir. Sick and near death,
132 Henry then learned that his favourite son **John** had also taken sides against him. Muttering 'shame, shame on a conquered king' he died soon after - a poor reward for a good reign.

Henry III

Medieval monarch who made a mess of things

1207-72, KING OF ENGLAND (PLANTAGENET)

Henry III reigned for fifty-six mainly miserable years, coming to the throne aged nine on the death of his father King **John** in 1216. His biggest success was rebuilding Westminster Abbey. Through greed and favouritism he turned almost all his nobles against him, including his former friend **Simon de Montfort**. In 1261 the nobles rebelled. Led by Simon they defeated Henry at the Battle of Lewes (1264), breaking his power for ever. The rebellion was crushed by Henry's son, the future **Edward I**. Henry lived on for another eight years, a broken man.

132

158

75

Henry IV
"Bolingbroke"

He grabbed the crown and clung to it

1366-1413, KING OF ENGLAND (HOUSE OF LANCASTER)

Friends of Henry IV, also called Bolingbroke, thought he was too merciful to his enemies - it all depends what you mean by mercy. He was the first king of the House of Lancaster and fought his way to the throne in 1399, forcing **Richard II** to give up the crown. Richard was starved to death four months later.

Henry's life and troubled fourteen-year reign are described in **Shakespeare's** plays: *Henry IV Part I, Henry IV Part II* and *Richard II.* Shakespeare makes much of Henry's quarrel with Percy, Earl of Northumberland and Percy's son **Hotspur**, whom Henry killed at the Battle of Shrewsbury in 1403.

In later years he suffered from epilepsy.

Henry V
"Prince Hal"

He bashed the French

1387-1422, KING OF ENGLAND (HOUSE OF LANCASTER)

Henry, also known as Prince Hal, was very wild when young - or so it's said. He was also a brave soldier: when only fifteen he was wounded in the face by an arrow at the Battle of Shrewsbury, and he once challenged a French knight to single combat.

In 1413 when his father **Henry IV** was sick, he crept into the King's chamber and stole the crown. Then a few days later Henry IV died and Prince Hal became King Henry V of England. From that day on he stopped his wild ways, ruled wisely and lived simply. A brilliant general, he shared the hardships of his soldiers. At the

Battle of Agincourt in 1415, his small army overwhelmingly defeated the massed knights of France, mainly due to the skill of the English bowmen.

In fact much of his reign was spent fighting to win the crown of France and he eventually married Catherine de Valois, a daughter of the French King, and became heir to the French throne.

But he never won that throne, dying of an illness while on campaign in 1422.

Henry VI
"Royal-Saint"

Measly monarch who lost his grip

1421-71, KING OF ENGLAND (HOUSE OF LANCASTER)

Henry VI became King of England in 1422, on the death of his father **Henry V**, when he was just nine months old. Two months later his grandfather Charles VI of France also died and Henry was declared king of France (by the English). Not bad for a baby.

117

With a start like that things can only go downhill. During Henry's reign the English were driven out of France (except Calais) by the young French heroine, Joan of Arc, thus losing the Hundred Years' War. In 1455, Henry was taken prisoner by the Duke of York at the Battle of St Albans, which started the Wars of the Roses* (1455-85). A quiet, religious man and a useless king, Henry was probably murdered on the orders of the next king, **Edward IV**.

78

Henry VII

He stopped the Middle Ages and started the Tudors

1457-1509, KING OF ENGLAND (TUDOR)

Henry VII was the first Tudor king of England. His victory over **Richard III** at the Battle of Bosworth in 1485 saw an end to the Wars of the Roses* (between followers of the red rose of York and the white rose of Lancaster) and is often thought of as marking the end of the Middle Ages too.

Henry was cool, crafty and careful with money. He used to read and sign almost every line of the royal accounts. A Lancastrian, he healed the wounds of the Wars of the Roses by marrying **Elizabeth of York**, daughter of **Edward IV** of York. When he came to the throne England was a weak and divided country. By the time he died, England was peaceful and prosperous.

Henry VIII

Big man who married a lot

1491-1547, KING OF ENGLAND (TUDOR)

119 Henry VIII, younger son of **Henry VII**, was big and he got bigger. When he came to the throne in 1509 he was tall, strong and athletic. By the time he died he was hugely fat and constipated and had to be hauled up and down stairs with a winch.

A big man, he did big things. Biggest were: the start of the Church of England (1531) and the Disssolution of the Monasteries (1536 and 1539), when he closed down the monasteries and took their money. He had six wives 41 (one after the other): **Catherine of Aragon**, **Anne** 24 **Boleyn**, Jane Seymour, Anne of Cleves, Catherine Howard and Catherine Parr. What happened to them is best remembered by the ryhme: 'Divorced, beheaded, died - divorced, beheaded, survived'.

79, 150 Henry's three royal children, **Edward VI**, **Mary** and 85 **Elizabeth I**, each ruled the country in their turn. Although often described as a monster because he executed two of his wives, Henry was actually quite popular with his people.

Hereward the Wake

Saxon hero who held up the Normans

active **1070-71**

235 Hereward the Wake (meaning 'The Watchful') was a Saxon rebel who held out against **William the Conqueror** after the Norman conquest of England following the Battle of Hastings (1066).

Hereward's base was on the Isle of Ely, an area of dry land in the middle of the east Cambridgeshire marshes. In 1070, he joined forces with a fleet of Danes, whom William had allowed to stay nearby over the winter. Together Danes and Saxons sacked Peterborough, taking treasure from Peterborough monastery. The Danes left for Denmark shortly after, leaving Hereward and his followers to face the wrath of William. William captured Ely in 1071 and most of the Saxon rebels surrendered. Hereward escaped - out of history and into legend.

Herschel, Sir Frederick William

He discovered the planet Uranus

1738-1822

In 1781, William Herschel discovered the planet Uranus, the first new planet to be discovered since ancient times. He did it with a powerful telescope which he made himself.

He was a German musician who moved to England and there became interested in the stars. Unable to afford a big telescope, he set out to make his own, grinding his own reflecting mirrors. He was so keen to make the best possible telescope that he threw away two hundred mirrors before he was satisfied and once spent sixteen hours without a break polishing a mirror to perfection.

Herschel made many other discoveries apart from Uranus. He had ideas about galaxies and the universe which were way ahead of his time. He died at the age of eighty-four years - which happens to be the length of time taken by Uranus to circle the Sun.

Hogarth, William

Artist who told tales

1697-1764

William Hogarth was born and bred a Londoner. Bits of eighteenth century London found their way into his most famous prints and paintings.

Hogarth liked to tell stories with his paintings. Usually there's an unhappy ending. Series of paintings such as *The Good and Idle Apprentices*, *A Harlot's Progress*, *A Rake's Progress* and *Marriage à la Mode* show what happens to people who are lazy or greedy or both. Hogarth was neither. His paintings and prints are absolutely crammed full of action. Like the 'Good Apprentice' he earned his fame and fortune.

Hore-Belisha, Leslie

He brought us beacons

1893-1957

Yes, 'Belisha' as in 'Belisha beacon'. As Transport Minister from 1934, he introduced driving tests for new drivers and the round, flashing, amber lights beside zebra crossings. In 1940 he resigned as Minister at the War Office, worried that Hitler's German army would pierce British defences in France - four months later he was proved right.

Horsa *see* **Hengist**

Hotspur
(Sir Henry Percy)

Noble knight who messed with monarchs

1364-1403

198 Hotspur was a mighty warrior (and a hero in **Shakespeare's** play *Henry IV, Part 1*). He was given his nickname by the Scots because of the tireless way he guarded the border between Scotland and England in the 1380s.

116 Hotspur was almost exactly the same age as **Henry IV**, whom he and his father, the Earl of Northumberland, helped to the throne in 1399. In 1403, father and son fell out with Henry. Hotspur gathered an army and marched to defeat Henry at Shrewsbury. But Henry was ready for him. In the battle which followed, Hotspur and thirty knights fought their way to the King's banner. They killed someone dressed in Henry's armour, but it wasn't the King.

It was Hotspur who died that day, not Henry - Henry is said to have wept tears over his body.

Howard, Catherine *see* **Henry VIII**

Howard, Charles
Lord Howard of Effingham

Top Tudor admiral who crushed the Spanish Armada

1536-1624

Charles Howard was a Tudor nobleman, first cousin
85 once removed of Queen **Elizabeth I** herself. As such
(and because he was handsome) he got the top jobs. In
1587, Elizabeth ordered him to prepare the English
army and navy for a Spanish invasion, which might
happen any day.

So Howard was Commander-in-Chief of the British
fleet when the Spanish Armada sailed slowly up the
English Channel one summer's day in 1588. His council
71 of war included brilliant seamen such as **Sir Francis**
92 **Drake** and **Martin Frobisher**. The Spanish fleet was
larger but Howard was a careful commander. Expert
English captains picked off the Spanish ships one by
one until the Armada was weakened, and then the
remainder was crushed. Only a broken fragment of the
Armada escaped back to Spain.

Howard, John

Pasty-faced prison reformer

1726-90

John Howard was a short, skinny, pasty-faced vegetarian who didn't drink. But although he was feeble on the outside, he had a will of iron on the inside.

In 1773, he was made High Sheriff of Bedfordshire and became aware of the terrible state of Bedford Jail. The place was filthy and the jailers were paid by the prisoners, as if prison was some sort of ghastly hotel. Those who couldn't pay had to stay inside until they did - even if they'd been found not guilty at their trial. Howard set off on a tour of other British prisons and found that most were just as bad as Bedford, if not worse. He persuaded Parliament to pass two acts, one to make prisons cleaner, the other to make sure that jailers were properly paid (1774).

Howard spent the rest of his life campaigning to make prisons better. The Howard League for Prison Reform (founded 1866) is named after him. It aims to improve modern prison conditions.

Inglis, Elsie Maud

Doctor who fought for women's rights

1864-1917

Elsie Inglis was one of the first female medical students in Edinburgh. She was shocked by the attitude of many male doctors towards women doctors at that time and by the lack of hospital care for women in childbirth. So in 1892 she started a medical school for women and in 1901 she started a hospital for women in childbirth, staffed by women only. In her spare time she campaigned for women's right to vote, founding the Scottish Women's Suffragette Federation in 1906.

After World War I broke out in 1914 she started three military hospitals in Serbia. She was forced to leave in 1916 but was back in Europe again within the year helping wounded soldiers in Russia. Her health failed in the bitter cold. Forced to leave Europe yet again in 1917 after the Russian Revolution had started, she died shortly after in Britain. She never married - from the looks of it, this brave woman didn't have the time.

Jack the Ripper

Vicious Victorian murderer

active 1888

In 1888 the London police received hand-written notes from a man who signed himself 'Jack the Ripper'. 'Jack' mocked the police for failing to catch a vicious murderer (himself) who stalked the streets of Whitechapel in London's East End.

In an orgy of terror Jack killed his women victims by cutting their throats. He knew a little about human anatomy and used to mutilate their bodies, once posting half a kidney to the police. No one has ever discovered his real identity. One theory is that he was the Duke of Clarence, cousin of Queen **Victoria**.

223

James I and VI
"The wisest fool in Christendom"

Good king of Scotland, and not a fool either

1566-1625, KING OF ENGLAND & SCOTLAND (STUART)

James was as Scottish as haggis and Scotch whisky. He was the son of **Mary Queen of Scots**, who was beheaded on the orders of **Elizabeth I**. But whereas Mary had been brought up in France, James was

151
85

brought up in Scotland and was a Scotsman through and through.

After his mother's execution he stayed friendly with Elizabeth, partly for the money she sent him but also because she was very clever and gave him good advice. She made him the heir to her kingdom and when she died in 1603, he travelled south to become King of both Scotland and England.

He was never very popular in England where the English didn't care for his Scottish advisors and disliked his ideas for uniting the two kingdoms. Far from being 'the wisest fool in Christendom' as was said of him, he was in fact one of the best kings Scotland ever had, as well as being a good scholar.

James II and VII

He lost his throne

1633-1701, KING OF ENGLAND AND SCOTLAND (STUART)

In 1664, an English fleet sailed into the harbour of Dutch New Amsterdam in America and captured the city. It was renamed 'New York' after James Duke of York, Lord High Admiral and younger brother of **Charles II**.

49

James was a good Lord High Admiral, but in 1685 he became king James II. He was a lousy king. The problem was that around 1668 he'd become a Catholic*. Most of his subjects were Protestants*. They didn't trust him and he didn't trust them. In 1688 in the 'Glorious Revolution' his subjects invited William of Orange to come to Britain to replace him. William accepted their invitation and became **William III**. He allowed James to escape to France.

James II was the last Stuart* king. He tried once to get his crown back: by invading Ireland in 1689. He was defeated by William at the Battle of the Boyne - and that was the end of that.

James IV

He failed at Flodden

1473-1513, KING OF SCOTLAND (STUART)

James was a strong king who united Scotland and was the last Scottish king to speak the ancient Gaelic 119 language. He married Margaret, daughter of **Henry VII** of England in 1503, and it was due to this marriage that 128 England and Scotland were finally united under the Stuart king **James I/VI** in 1603. He died at the Battle of Flodden when a large Scottish army was destroyed by the English.

James V

Mediocre monarch

1512-42, KING OF SCOTLAND (STUART)

This is a story of baby monarchs. James V became King of Scotland when only a year old on the death of his

father **James IV.** His successor, the disastrous **Mary Queen of Scots**, was only a *week* old when she became Queen after him. For the first twenty-eight years of James' reign, Scotland wallowed in chaos while nobles fought for power, although later he brought some order to the kingdom. James died after being defeated by the English at the Battle of Solway Firth. The lesson for Scotland? Baby monarchs are best avoided.

Jenner, Edward

Doctor who conquered smallpox

1749-1823

Smallpox is a deadly disease. Large numbers of people used to die of it every year. Almost worse, those that survived were often 'pockmarked', their faces hideously ravaged with scars. Many feared this more than death.

For hundreds of years, the Turks and the Chinese had known that a mild dose of the disease would protect the sufferer from a more deadly attack. Jenner, an English doctor, heard of a tradition that people who had had cowpox (which is less dangerous) didn't catch smallpox. In 1796, he infected a small boy called James Phipps with cowpox, which James duly caught. Two months later he infected him with smallpox, which James didn't catch (fortunately!).

Jenner called his new technique 'vaccination' after *vaccinia*, the Latin for cowpox. By 1805, the number of deaths from smallpox in Britain was down by two thirds.

John "Lackland"

Tough medieval monarch nearly nobbled by his nobles

1167-1216, KING OF ENGLAND (PLANTAGENET)

115 King John was given the nickname 'Lackland' by his father **Henry II**, who left all royal lands to his elder sons and none to John, the youngest. Much of John's life was spent trying to put this right - as he saw it.

197
194 John is the bad king in the **Robin Hood** stories. His brother **Richard I**, the Lionheart, is the good king. In 1193, while Richard was returning from a crusade* John tried to seize the kingdom (1193), but had to give it up when Richard returned. He finally came to the throne in 1199 on Richard's death, but then fell out with his barons. They rebelled, forcing him to sign the Magna Carta (Great Charter) which limited the power of the crown (1215).

War between barons and king broke out again soon after. John was near defeat when he died of a fever at Newark, brought on by eating too many peaches and drinking a new type of beer.

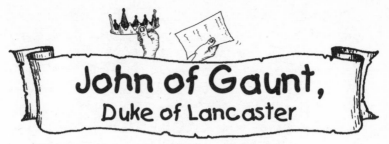

John of Gaunt,
Duke of Lancaster

Ancestor of kings

1340-99

John of Gaunt was a powerful medieval nobleman. His name comes from Ghent in Belgium where he was born. He was the fourth son of **Edward III**.

77

He's most important for who's descended from him. In 1359, John married Blanche of Lancaster and he was made Duke of Lancaster three years later. Their son Bolingbroke became **Henry IV**, the first Lancastrian King of England. The Tudors are descended from another son, John Beaufort, by his third wife, Catherine Swynford, whom he married in 1396. (She was sister-in-law of the poet **Chaucer**.)

116

51

Johnson, Amy
"Queen of the Air"

Record-breaking pilot who flew to fame

1903-41

Amy Johnson became a pilot in 1928. Two years later she set out to beat the world record for a solo flight from

England to Darwin, Australia. Her plane was a tiny Moth aircraft. She failed to beat the record by three days but the trip made her famous and the papers crowned her 'Queen of the Air'. Other solo trips followed, to South Africa and Japan among other places. At the outbreak of World War II she joined the Air Transport Auxiliary and was lost bailing out over the Thames Estuary, while 'ferrying a plane with material for the air ministry' as the official account of the tragedy rather mysteriously puts it.

Johnson, Samuel
"Dr Johnson"

Writer who talked a lot

1709-84

Most people thought Dr Johnson was an idiot when they first met him. He was big and bumbling and very odd.

They soon changed their minds once he started talking. Johnson was one of the great 'wits' of eighteenth century London. He was brilliantly funny and very clever and his many friends loved him for it. He ruled the world of writers like a great big bull. Along with plays, poems and other articles, he wrote a famous dictionary (published in 1755). Johnson's *Dictionary* was the first proper English dictionary.

However the work he's most famous for wasn't written by him at all, but by a young Scottish friend called James Boswell. Boswell's *Life of Samuel Johnson* is a masterpiece; it tells us as much about Boswell as about his large, likeable friend.

Jonson, Ben

Poet with attitude

1572-1637

Ben Jonson was a fighter as well as a writer. When a soldier in Flanders, he challenged a Spaniard to single combat and killed him. Later he killed a fellow actor in a duel, went to prison and was branded. Branding was done with a red-hot iron. The iron was held against the skin, leaving a scar such as 'M' for murderer.

198 Jonson was one of the greatest playwrights of his time after **Shakespeare**, who was a friend. In fact Shakespeare is said to have been an actor in Jonson's first known comedy *Every Man in His Humour* (1598). Further brilliant plays such as *Volpone* and *Bartholomew Fair* soon followed. They're still good to watch today and contain beautiful poems such as *Drink to me only with thine eyes* (in *Volpone*).

128 In the reign of **James I** he put on popular shows (called Masques) for the court, but then life grew harder. In 1632 he wrote 'Come leave the loathed Stage' to show how fed up he was. Despite setbacks, at the time of his death he was a hero to many young writers.

Keats, John

Romantic poet who died young

1795-1821

John Keats, one of England's greatest poets, died of consumption (tuberculosis, a disease of the lungs) in Rome when he was only twenty-five. He was on a walking tour in the north of England when he caught the illness. Up to that time he'd been strong and lively. (He once beat a butcher in a stand-up fight.) Far from being 'writ in water', the words he suggested for his tombstone, his name will be remembered for a long time, alongside poets such as **Shelley** and **Byron**.

200, 35

His most famous work was a small book called *Lamia ... and Other Poems*, published in 1820, which included: *Ode on a Grecian Urn*, *To a Nightingale* and *To Autumn*. By the time it was published, Keats probably knew that he was going to die. His journey to Italy in September of that year was a last desperate attempt to shake off the illness.

Kipling, Rudyard

Writer of *The Jungle Book*

1865-1936

Rudyard Kipling was an imperialist: he believed in 'Empire', that it was the duty of Europeans, Englishmen in particular, to rule the world and teach other people European civilization. That's not fashionable nowadays but it was widely believed then.

Imperialism didn't stop his interest in Indian life, where he was born and where he spent nine years as a journalist (1880-89). Kipling set his famous *Jungle Book* stories, on which the Walt Disney film is based, in the Indian jungle. (There were actually two *Jungle Books*, published 1894-5.) His famous book, *Kim*, is about the adventures of a little Indian boy. Other wonderful books are the *Just So Stories* and *Puck of Pook's Hill*. Whatever you think of his opinions, he's still a good read today.

Kitchener, Horatio Herbert
"Lord Kitchener of Khartoum"

World War I general - and poster
1850-1916

Kitchener was Commander-in-Chief of a combined British/Arab army which smashed Sudanese forces at the Battle of Omdurman in 1898. The Sudanis stood no chance against British machine guns. This made him a national hero. (The 'Khartoum' which he became 'Lord' of is the capital of Sudan.) He then led the British forces in South Africa during the Second Boer War (1899-1902), which made him even more of a hero.

When World War I started in 1914, who better to make Secretary of State for War than Kitchener? He asked for volunteers to enlist in brand new 'Kitchener' armies - his recruiting poster, a picture of himself and the words: 'YOUR COUNTRY NEEDS YOU', is famous to this day. Without him, Britain and France might well have lost the war. He was difficult to work with however; his fellow ministers were glad when he left on a mission to Russia in June 1916 - which is not to say they were glad when his ship was sunk by a German mine shortly after.

Knox, John

Scottish Protestant preacher

around 1505-72

When John Knox was born, Scotland was still a Catholic* country; by the time he died it was Protestant*- mainly due to him.

Like his country he started out Catholic. So he knew what his enemy was like and he knew he was in for a fight. The fight included: eighteen months as a prisoner on a French ship (1547-9), several years in exile (1549-59 on and off), and fierce arguments with the rulers of his day. In 1558, he published his *First Blast of the Trumpet Against the Monstrous Regiment of Women* aimed at the then (female) rulers of Scotland, England and France. Unfortunately it appeared at the very moment that another woman, the Protestant **Elizabeth I**, became Queen of England and she never forgave him.

85

In 1560, poor Catholic **Mary Queen of Scots** arrived in Scotland to take up her crown. She was no match for Knox - or Elizabeth. Seven years later, Mary was a prisoner in England and Protestantism had triumphed.

151

Latimer, Bishop Hugh

Protestant bishop who burned for his beliefs

around 1485-1555

120 Hugh Latimer was Protestant* - very Protestant. **Henry VIII** liked him because he helped Henry get rid of his
41 old Catholic* wife, **Catherine of Aragon**. Latimer then became chaplain to Henry's new Protestant wife, **Anne**
24 **Boleyn**. He was in fact rather too Protestant for Henry and twice ended up in the Tower of London.

He was also Protestant enough to send Catholics to burn at the stake - and Protestant enough to be burned
150 himself once Henry's Catholic daughter **Mary** became queen. He and Bishop Ridley were burned at Oxford on 16 October 1555. Ridley's brother tied a bag of gunpowder to each of their necks so that they would die quickly. When the flames were lit, Latimer encouraged Ridley with the famous words: 'Be of good comfort, Master Ridley. We shall this day light such a candle, by God's grace, in England as I trust shall never be put out.'

Lawrence, TE (Thomas Edward)
"Lawrence of Arabia"

World War I fighter for Arab freedom

1888-1935

During World War I, Arabia was part of the fading Turkish Empire. The Arabs wanted independence and, since Turkey was allied to Germany, Britain helped the Arabs to fight the Turks. From 1916, Lawrence commanded a force of desert Arabs. They blew up Turkish trains and railway lines thus paralysing the Turkish garrison at Medina in modern Saudi Arabia. In 1917, the Turks offered a reward of £20,000 for the capture of 'Al Urans (Lawrence), Destroyer of Engines'.

Lawrence, a scholar and British intelligence officer, lived like an Arab. He spoke Arabic, wore Arab clothes and shared all the hardships of his men. In 1918, he captured Damascus and held it for three days until the regular British army arrived. His adventures are told in his masterpiece, *The Seven Pillars of Wisdom* which was first printed 1926.

When the war ended, he was tired out. He retreated from fame and joined the RAF under a false name. He later died in a motorcycle accident in Dorset, after swerving to avoid two boys on bicycles.

Lister, Joseph, Lord

Enemy of germs who started antiseptic surgery

1827-1912

In 1853 Joseph Lister, a young English doctor, became a house surgeon at Edinburgh Royal Infirmary. He was horrified by the number of patients whose wounds became infected and went rotten.

At that time no one knew what caused infection. It wasn't until 1865 that Lister heard about the great French scientist, Louis Pasteur. Pasteur had discovered that diseases are caused by tiny living things, now called 'germs'. Suddenly it was obvious: kill the 'germs' in wounds and the wounds won't get infected. To start with, Lister used carbolic acid as the most effective germ-killer - or 'antiseptic'. He dressed wounds with carbolic, he soaked bandages in it and he even sprayed the air around an operating table using a special carbolic spray device. He then went on to find ways of improving on pure carbolic.

The result: there were a lot less rotting wounds than there used to be, and deaths fell dramatically. Thanks to Joseph Lister, surgery would never be the same again.

Livingstone, David

Victorian missionary and explorer in Africa

1813-73

David Livingstone made three great journeys across the centre of Africa. He was the first European to see the Victoria Falls among other places. He believed that what Africa needed was Christianity and trade - but not the slave trade. As a Scottish missionary, he could provide the Christianity, trade would follow his explorations - and he would do his best to stop the slave trade.

207

His last journey (1866-73) was meant to discover the source of the Nile. It was the toughest of the lot. Years passed with no word of him and eventually **Henry Morton Stanley** was sent to bring him back. At Ujiji on the banks of Lake Tanganyika, Stanley is said to have met Livingstone with the words, 'Doctor Livingstone, I presume.' But Livingstone never would return home. He pressed on, though he was so sick he had to be carried on a litter.

Livingstone died at Chitambo (in modern Zambia). His African followers buried his heart but wrapped his body in bark and sent it back to Britain.

Llewelyn ap Gruffydd

Welsh warrior and freedom fighter

died 1282

Llewelyn ap Gruffydd was a great champion of Welsh freedom from English rule. He was a grandson of **Llewelyn the Great** (see below) and by 1254 had made himself ruler of all Wales. His life was spent fighting, first against **Henry III** and then against the mighty **Edward I**. After Llewelyn was killed in 1282, Edward caged Wales in a great ring of castles which still stand to this day.

116
75

Llewelyn the Great

He carved out a kingdom

died 1240, KING OF WALES

Llewelyn was brought up in England, but returned to Wales to carve out a kingdom for himself in the north, taking advantage of troubles in England during the reign of **John**. Later south Wales also submitted to him. During the boyhood of **Henry III** he was driven out of the south again but kept a firm hold on the north. He spent his last year in a monastery.

132
116

Lloyd George, David

Prime Minister of pensions

1863-1945

Lloyd George was a Welshman. He never forgot his childhood on a farm in Wales.

As Chancellor of the Exchequer in 1908, he started Britain's first national insurance and pensions schemes. For the first time, British working-class people could get help from the government when suffering from bad health, old age or unemployment.

Then in 1916 he became Prime Minister - during the second half of the First World War. He hated the horrors of trench warfare but led Britain's war effort nevertheless. At the height of his power in 1921, he agreed to the treaty which gave independence to southern Ireland - and at the next election he was voted out of office because of it. He lived on until almost the end of the Second World War.

Locke, John

1632-1704, PHILOSOPHER

In his great book, *An Essay Concerning Human Understanding* (published 1690), John Locke argued that at birth our minds are a blank sheet, without thoughts or ideas, although he did accept that we're born with individual personalities.

He himself had plenty of personality - he needed it. He lived through the Civil War, the beheading of **Charles I**, the 'Restoration' of **Charles II** and the 'Glorious Revolution' of 1688 which expelled **James II**, and during all that time he kept to his beliefs in democracy and religious toleration - except for Catholics* who he thought were too intolerant!

48
49
129

Chiefly Locke is famous as a pioneer of empiricism, the idea that everything we know is based on experience and that all ideas and scientific theories must be tested by looking at the real world. This philosophy has lain behind all the scientific and industrial revolutions of the modern world.

MacAlpin, Kenneth

died around **858**, KING OF THE SCOTS

In 834, Kenneth became king of the Scots in the west of Scotland. Seven years later he drove out the Vikings and by 846 had made himself King of both the Picts, who lived in the east and north, and of the Scots. His new kingdom of Alban was the first to unite Scotland north of the River Forth.

Macbeth

Bad king - good play

around **1005-1057**, KING OF SCOTLAND

198 As well as being a play by **Shakespeare**, Macbeth was a

real-life medieval warrior. In 1040 he rebelled against his cousin, King Duncan I, killing him in battle - not in bed as Shakespeare says. Having ruled in Duncan's place for fourteen years Macbeth was forced out of Cumbria (then part of Scotland) by the Earl of Northumbria on the 'Day of the Seven Sleepers'. Three years later Duncan's son **Malcolm III** finished him off at the Battle of Lumphanan.

Macdonald, James Ramsay

First Labour Prime Minister

1866-1937

The modern Labour Party* was started in 1900 (first called the Labour Representation Committee) and Ramsay Macdonald was its first Prime Minister. Not bad for the son of a poor Scots ploughman, born in a tiny two-room cottage. It wasn't luck that got him there: he was clever and very hard working. (Even as Prime Minister he was known to look up train times for his secretaries.)

He entered Parliament in the same year as the Labour parliamentary party started. By 1922, he'd been chosen to be party leader and two years later he found himself Prime Minister after a general election. This first taste of power only lasted two years, but from 1929-31 he led a Labour government and from 1931-5, he led a joint government of Labour, Liberals and Tories.

Malcolm III
"Canmore (Great Head)"

The first king to rule all Scotland

around 1031-1093, KING OF SCOTLAND

146 Malcolm came to the throne in 1057 having killed his father's murderer, **Macbeth**. Like many early kings, he was a fierce warrior but he couldn't read or write.

73
235 Much of his life was spent fighting the Normans who conquered England in 1066. Trouble started in 1067 when he gave shelter to **Edgar the Ætheling**, Saxon heir to the English throne. In 1072, **William the Conqueror** invaded Scotland, Malcolm was forced to become William's 'man' and Edgar was no longer welcome at Malcolm's court.

237 Troubles continued and each side was as ruthless as the other. In 1092, Malcolm quarrelled with William the Conqueror's son, **William II**. He was killed in an ambush in Northumberland at a place still called 'Malcolm's Cross'.

Marlborough, Duke of *see* Churchill, John

Marlowe, Christopher

Terrific Tudor playwright
1564-93

Christopher Marlowe died young. On 30 May 1593 he was stabbed following an argument in a lodging house in Deptford. The blow was probably to the eye, 'his brains coming out at the dagger point' as one later description puts it.

Marlowe was only twenty-nine when he died but he packed more into those few short years than gets done in a hundred lesser lives. His first play *Tamburlaine the Great*, produced in 1587 just six years before his death, changed the face of Tudor theatre. After that he wrote *The Tragical History of Doctor Faustus*, *The Jew of Malta*, *Edward II* and other masterpieces. He also wrote beautiful poems such as: *Come live with me and be my love*. He's the only poet to be quoted word for word by **Shakespeare** (in *As You Like It*). On top of all this, he probably worked for **Elizabeth I's** secret service.

198
85

At the time of his death Marlowe's enemies had accused him of atheism and blasphemy. A warrant was out for his arrest. Not believing in God was a serious crime in those days - if the Deptford dagger hadn't got him, the government probably would have.

Mary I
"Bloody Mary"

Catholic queen who burned bishops

1516-58, QUEEN OF ENGLAND AND IRELAND (TUDOR)

120
41
79

Mary was the eldest daughter of **Henry VIII**, by his first wife **Catherine of Aragon**. When she came to the throne on the death of her brother **Edward VI** in 1553, she was already thirty-seven years old. She had worn features, no eyebrows, a strangely deep voice - and (apart from some rejoicing at the coronation) not many people liked her. Being a staunch Catholic* she then married Philip II, King of Spain, the most powerful Catholic in Europe. Not many people liked Spain either.

140,
59

Mary was determined to turn Protestant* England into a Catholic country, and she was ready to use force to make it happen. In the three years before she died more than 300 Protestants were burned at the stake, including the bishops Ridley, **Latimer** and **Cranmer**. Hence her nickname 'Bloody Mary'.

Poor Mary, England didn't become Catholic and she became even more unpopular. Even her husband didn't like her. She died of sickness, and perhaps of sadness.

Mary II

The 'Mary' in 'William and Mary'

1662-94, QUEEN OF GREAT BRITAIN (STUART)

129 Mary was the daughter of **James II**. Unlike her Catholic* father she was a Protestant.* In 1677, she married William of Orange, the champion of Protestant
238 Europe and the future **William III** of Great Britain. In 1688 when her husband was invited to England in the 'Glorious Revolution' to replace her father, she stood by her husband. 'William and Mary' shared the throne between them.

Mary Queen of Scots

Beautiful woman, lousy queen, Catholic hero

1542-87, QUEEN OF SCOTLAND (STUART)

Mary was just a week old when she became Queen on
130 the death of her father, **James V** of Scotland. She'd lived

in France from the age of six, so she was really French when she came to Scotland to rule in 1561. Also she was a Catholic* and her subjects were mostly Protestant*.

Mary was beautiful and clever but her reign was a disaster. It involved the murder of one husband, Lord Darnley, marriage to her husband's suspected murderer, the Earl of Bothwell, imprisonment, and finally flight and exile in England (1567).

Her biggest problem wasn't Scottish at all however: it was English and it was called **Elizabeth I**. Unfortunately Mary had a claim on the English crown through her grandfather **Henry VII**. Lots of English Catholics wanted to see her on the English throne in place of Protestant Elizabeth. Elizabeth kept Mary a prisoner for years while Catholic plots stewed and simmered. Twenty years after Mary first arrived in England, Elizabeth finally ordered her execution.

Matilda
"Empress Maud"

She was kept from the crown
1102-67

Matilda had it all: she had beauty, noble blood and riches. There was just one problem - she was a woman. When she was seven, her father, the mighty **Henry I**, arranged for her to marry the German Emperor Henry V - the Emperor was then thirty-seven. That's how she became 'Empress' Maud. He died in 1125 and her father then married her to Geoffrey of Anjou. By now she was twenty-six - Geoffrey was fifteen.

Meanwhile Matilda's father had forced the English barons to agree that she should succeed him on the English throne. Fat hope - a woman on the throne - it was unheard of! When Henry I died in 1135, the barons backed **Stephen** for king and a bitter civil war followed. Matilda showed that she was brave enough to be her warrior father's daughter. Among other adventures she escaped from Oxford Castle during a siege. In a white robe and with three white-robed companions she fled across a frozen river and through the middle of Stephen's camp in the snow.

But she didn't win the war and she was never crowned Queen of England.

Maxwell, James Clerk

Scientist who discovered electromagnetic radiation

1831-79

When James Maxwell was young, his teacher thought he was stupid and his fellow pupils called him 'dafty'. How wrong they were! By the time he was fifteen he'd written a mathematical paper good enough to be published by the Royal Society of Edinburgh.

He went on to become perhaps the most important
169 scientist since **Sir Isaac Newton**. He's specially famous because he developed the theory of 'electromagnetic
89 radiation', based on **Michael Faraday's** ideas. He proved that an electromagnet field radiates out from its source at a constant speed of roughly 299,792.5 kilometres per second - the speed of light. Maxwell also suggested that light was a form of electromagnetic radiation.

Merlin

Mythical magician - maybe

active around **500**

11 In popular legend Merlin is an adviser to King **Arthur**. But in ancient Welsh legend there are at least two

Merlins: *Merlin Emrys*, Arthur's adviser, and *Merlin Wyllt* who lived a hundred years later and was real. It may be that the real Merlin Wyllt was muddled with the legendary Merlin Emrys when the Arthur stories were being written. Another possibility is that he's based on an adviser to the British king **Vortigern**, the king who invited the first Saxon conquerors into Britain. Be that as it may, a Welsh triad (an early type of poem) says that he went to sea in a glass boat and was never heard of again.

224

Milton, John

Puritan poet who wrote *Paradise Lost*
1608-74

John Milton was a Puritan*. As a Puritan, he backed the Puritan Parliament in the Civil War which ended with the execution of **Charles I** in 1649.

48

Milton believed in freedom (although not for the king). In 1644 he wrote a famous poem, the 'Areopagitica', which argued that everyone should be free to publish what they want without asking for permission. He continued to work for Parliament right up until **Charles II** was restored to the throne in 1660. By that time he'd gone blind and had started his great work *Paradise Lost.* This long poem tells how the human race fell from God's favour and how Adam and Eve were driven from Paradise.

49

Charles II pardoned Milton even though he'd supported the execution of Charles's father. He let Milton live out the rest of his days in peace.

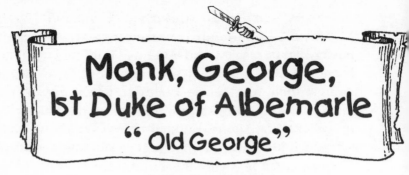

Monk, George, 1st Duke of Albemarle
"Old George"

1608-70, SOLDIER

George Monk was a clever, careful general who worked for **Oliver Cromwell** during the Commonwealth when Britain had no king. After Cromwell died, Monk decided it would be best for Britain if the monarchy were restored and **Charles II** took his seat on the throne. Without Monk's powerful support, the 'Restoration' of 1660 might not have happened at all.

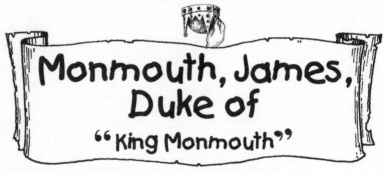

Monmouth, James, Duke of
"King Monmouth"

Protestant claimant to the throne
1649-85

James, Duke of Monmouth, was beheaded on Tower Hill on 15 July 1685 for starting a rebellion. It took five blows of the axe to finish him off and even then his head had to be cut from his body with a knife. In fact, it was almost harder to cut off his head than it was to crush his rebellion.

The story starts with a jumble of Jameses: James Monmouth had landed in Lyme Regis, just a month before, claiming to be the true King James II of England. His followers tended to call him 'King Monmouth' because there was already a **James II** on the throne. The real James II was a Catholic*; Monmouth was a Protestant*. He claimed the crown because he was the son of **Charles II** by one of Charles's many mistresses. The real James II was Charles II's brother.

129

49

Men flocked to join 'Monmouth's Rebellion' from all over the West Country. But they were no match for the government forces and were crushed. Monmouth fled but was found hiding in a ditch. His followers were hunted down and hanged in their hundreds in the 'Bloody Assize', the name given to the merciless trials which followed.

Montfort, Simon de, Earl of Leicester

"Simon the Righteous"

Medieval hero who planned a parliament

around 1208-1265

Simon de Montfort was a young Frenchman who became the most powerful nobleman in England. By 1238 when he was only twenty-eight, he was King **Henry III's** right-hand man, but later the two men quarrelled. Simon then took the lead in the 'Barons' Wars' against Henry, who was unpopular with his subjects. He defeated Henry at the Battle of Lewes (1264) and captured Henry's son, Prince Edward (the future **Edward I**). Simon now set out to reform the country, summoning a 'Model Parliament' which met in 1265. It was made up of 120 clergymen, 23 'lay' barons, 2 knights from each county and 2 citizens from each borough - the first time common citizens had been summoned. Our modern parliament has grown from this model.

Then Prince Edward escaped. At the Battle of Evesham (1265) Edward massacred Simon and a small force of his followers. Simon's mutilated body was buried in the Abbey of Evesham and his tomb became a place of pilgrimage for the common people. As for Edward, in 1295, now Edward I, he called his own parliament - modelled on Simon's.

Montgomery, Bernard Law,
Viscount Montgomery of Alamein
" Monty"

World War II general who bashed the Germans in North Africa

1887-1976

Montgomery was a skinny, sharp-faced, vain, little man; he was also honest and brave and one of the greatest British generals of World War II. He was a very careful general: he'd been wounded and left for dead during the slaughter of World War I and was determined that lives would not be wasted like that again.

53 In 1942, **Winston Churchill** chose him to be the commander of the British Eighth Army which had been badly bruised by the Germans in North Africa. Montgomery led the British to victory at the Battle of Alamein and went on to drive the Germans right out of Africa and into Italy. This success was the high point of his career.

He later commanded the allied ground forces in the 'D Day' invasion of Europe in 1944, although his prickly personality made it almost impossible for the Americans to work with him. He suffered his only defeat shortly after, at Arnhem in September 1944.

Montrose, James Graham, Marquis of

Scottish leader who supported Charles I

1612-50

Montrose was one of the Scottish leaders who in 1637 signed a 'Covenant' vowing to protect the Scottish Presbyterian (a type of Puritan*) religion against the Church of England of **Charles I**. A year later he changed sides. He became one of the best of Charles' generals, leading highland armies to victory after victory against the 'Covenanters'. Unfortunately his highland soldiers were brutal and the lowland Scots feared and despised them. Without the support of the lowlands, Montrose had no hope of winning Scotland. A year after his greatest victory at Kilsyth (1645), he had to flee to the Continent.

He was in Brussels when he heard news of the execution of Charles I. That same year he set sail for Scotland once more, but his small fleet was shipwrecked. Out of 1,200 men, only two hundred survived. This pitiful remnant was easily defeated and Montrose himself was hanged shortly after.

Moore, Sir John

Brave general who died at Coruña

1761-1809

In 1808 Sir John Moore took command of British forces in the Peninsular War against the French (part of the Napoleonic Wars). The French had 300,000 soldiers in Spain and the British force was less than 30,000 and Britain's Spanish allies were useless. Moore's situation was difficult, to put it mildly.

In December, he learned that Madrid had surrendered to the French leader Napoleon and that an army of 70,000 French soldiers had cut the British line of retreat into Portugal. Moore marched his army a roundabout route for 250 miles through mountainous country arriving at the port of Coruña on 13 January 1809. Three days later a French army attacked while the British were boarding their ships. In the battle which followed, the French were beaten, but Moore himself was killed by grapeshot which smashed his left shoulder. His burial in Coruña is remembered in the sad poem 'The Burial of Sir John Moore' by Charles Wolfe.

More, Sir Thomas
"a man for all seasons"

Friend of Henry VIII - for a while
1477-1535

120 **Henry VIII** really liked Thomas More. More was funny and clever. He wrote a popular book called *Utopia* about a country where people live peacefully and are free to disagree about religion. Henry used to call round to More's house uninvited for dinner and walk in the garden with his arm round More's shoulder. But More knew Henry better than Henry knew himself: 'If my head should win him a castle in France, it should not fail to go,' he told a friend, meaning that Henry would happily chop off More's head if he could gain from it.

His head *did* go - on 6 July 1535 it was chopped off, parboiled and stuck on a pole on London Bridge after conviction for high treason. Not that More *was* guilty of treason: he simply disagreed with Henry's decision to create the Church of England with Henry in charge, and 24 he opposed Henry's marriage to **Anne Boleyn**. As Lord Chancellor, More was just too important to be allowed to disagree with the King and get away with it.

Morgan, Sir Henry

Buccaneer who bashed the Spaniards

1635-88

When he was a boy, Morgan was taken to Barbados to be sold as a servant. Later he joined the buccaneers on the nearby island of Jamaica (a buccaneer is a type of pirate) and became a captain. By 1666 the buccaneers had chosen him to be their admiral.

For the next six years Morgan waged brutal war on the Spaniards, who wanted to take over Jamaica. The British authorities let him get on with it. They turned a blind eye on the behaviour of his buccaneers, who tortured prisoners to find out where treasure might be stored and generally behaved like drunken hooligans - which they were. Not that Morgan was any better. Eventually even the British were sickened by the buccaneers' brutality. Morgan was taken back to England in disgrace. But there he won the support of **George III** and was returned to Jamaica - as 'Lieutenant Governor'. Who said, 'crime doesn't pay'?

97

Morris, William

Victorian craftsman and socialist

1834-96

William Morris was a Victorian artist, writer, craftsman and socialist*. He believed that working people should enjoy their work. No bleak factories for Morris, he dreamed of a world of creative craftsmen.

That's how he tried to live himself. Throughout his life, designs for furniture, wallpaper, books and paintings poured from his pen. You can still buy William Morris wallpaper today. He was a founder of the Arts and Crafts movement and wrote about his ideas in books such as *The Earthly Paradise*, *The Dream of John Ball* and *News from Nowhere*.

Morris, William Richard, Viscount Nuffield

Car-maker of Cowley

1877-1963

William Richard Morris was the first person to mass-produce cars in Britain. He started out as a bicycle repair man, went on to design bikes, then motorbikes and in 1912 the first Morris Oxford car. It could go at 50 mph and cost £165. To cope with rising production he opened a car plant in the village of Cowley outside Oxford where he'd been brought up. In the slump of 1920-1 he slashed prices and his sales soared. By 1926, he was producing a third of all cars sold in Britain and was ready to widen his range. In 1930, he started the 'MG Motor Company' which made the famous MG sports car and in 1931 he produced the first Morris Minor - price £100.

Morris was generous as well as clever and hard-working. During his life he is thought to have given away more than 30 million pounds. He poured it into hospitals and charities. Most famous are Nuffield College Oxford and the Nuffield Foundation, founded in 1943 to further medical research. He was made Viscount Nuffield in 1938.

Mortimer, Roger de

Nasty nobleman who nobbled Ned

around 1287-1330

Roger de Mortimer was a powerful medieval nobleman and an ally of King **Edward II**. He held the coronation robes when Edward was crowned. Later he rebelled against Edward and was imprisoned in the Tower of London (1326), but he drugged his guards and escaped to France.

It was in France that he met up with Isabella, wife of Edward II, who was over on a mission from Edward. Isabella loathed her royal husband and fell madly in love with Mortimer. They decided to invade England, landing in September 1326. It was almost too easy: within a few months Edward had been captured and brutally murdered and the lovers placed Isabella's son, the boy king **Edward III**, on the throne - and under their power.

Mortimer and Isabella were unpopular rulers. In 1330, Edward III took power into his own hands. Mortimer was hung, drawn and quartered.

Mosley, Sir Oswald Ernald

Fascist who failed

1896-1980

Oswald Mosley was rich, handsome and charming. In fact he was *too* rich, *too* handsome and *too* charming. He thought he could do anything - even destroy British Parliamentary democracy*.

Having been in turn a Conservative, Liberal and Labour member of Parliament, in 1932 he formed the British Union of Fascists. Fascists don't believe in democracy. Their violent, anti-Jewish demonstrations soon drove away most supporters, leaving a band of vicious 'black-shirts'. When World War II with Fascist Germany broke out in 1939, Mosley was locked up together with his second wife.

After the war was over he tried for power one last time, forming the Union movement in 1948. It was a failure, as was he.

Nelson, Horatio, Viscount Nelson

Brave, one-eyed, British admiral

1758-1805

Horatio Nelson is one of Britain's best-loved heroes. He joined the navy when he was twelve, becoming an expert seaman and victor of great sea battles during the Napoleonic Wars against the French. He was incredibly brave and was often wounded. During the Battle of Copenhagen (1803) his commander raised the flags signalling 'discontinue action'. Nelson put his telescope to his blind eye (blinded in an earlier battle), joked that he couldn't see the flag - and kept on fighting. Typical.

He met his great love, Emma Hamilton, in 1793. Emma was the daughter of a blacksmith. She'd risen in the world due to her charm and beauty and had married the British Ambassador to Naples. She and Nelson became lovers after his triumph at the Battle of the Nile (1798). Her husband stayed friends with both of them.

Nelson was killed by a French musket shot during the Battle of Trafalgar off the coast of Spain, his last and greatest victory. His body was preserved in spirits and brought carefully back to Britain for a hero's funeral in St Paul's Cathedral.

Newcomen, Thomas

Inventor of the first really useful steam engine

1663-1729

Thomas Newcomen was either a Cornish ironmonger or blacksmith, no one's quite sure. Sometime before 1698, he started work on designs for a steam engine to pump water from Cornish tin mines. That year another British inventor, Captain Savery, patented his own design. Newcomen and Savery went into partnership and by 1712 Newcomen had built a much better engine, the Atmospheric Steam Engine. This used the condensation of steam to make a vacuum and then air pressure provided the power. By 1725, Newcomen's machine was widely used to pump mines and raise water for water wheels.

Newton, Sir Isaac

Scientist who discovered gravity

1642-1727

Isaac Newton is quite possibly the cleverest person who ever lived. His theory of 'Universal Gravitation' explained not only why the planets and the stars circle each other the way they do, but also why a pen will fall to the floor if you drop it. The basic idea came to him in 1666 while staying on his mother's farm to escape the plague. He saw an apple fall from a tree and - bingo! As if that wasn't enough, he also discovered that white light is made up of the colours of the rainbow, developed the first reflecting telescope and invented a form of differential calculus (a type of maths).

He was a modest man. 'If I have seen further than other men, it is because I stood on the shoulders of giants,' he said, speaking of the great scientists who'd gone before him. Well, a lot of other people were standing on giants' shoulders at the time - but they didn't see as far as Newton.

Niall of the Nine Hostages

Dark ages warrior

died 405

Niall had long yellow hair - typical of a Celtic chieftain of his day. He ruled at a time when the mighty Roman Empire was cracking under the strain of barbarian attacks. Niall was one of those barbarians. He fought in Britain and possibly in Gaul (modern France), as well as in his homeland of Ireland against rival 'kings'. He's chiefly famous because so many Irish tribes took their name from him, including the O'Neills and the O'Donnells. He's said to have been killed by one of his hostages, the son of the King of Leinster, probably off the coast of Gaul.

Nightingale, Florence
" the Lady of the Lamp"

Nurse who changed nursing

1820-1910

In Florence Nightingale's day, rich English girls were expected to do - almost nothing. Florence (so called after the town in Italy where she was born) couldn't bear the boredom of it. Instead, she became interested in hospitals and by 1853 was running a hospital in London.

Then in 1854 she was asked to go out to Turkey to manage the nursing of British soldiers wounded in the Crimean War (1854-56). Working up to twenty hours a day in the vast army hospital at Scutari, she transformed conditions for her soldier-patients. They called her the 'Lady of the Lamp' because she hardly took time off to sleep. No longer did they have to lie in blankets caked in blood and filth, eating rotten food. She made sure that there was a proper kitchen and good food, that there were bandages and clean, efficient nurses to put them on. Soon fewer soldiers were dying of wounds or illness.

Nursing became Florence's mission in life. Back in England she started schools for nurses and by the time she died at the age of ninety, nursing had become a respected profession - as it still is today.

Nuffield, Viscount *see* **Morris, William Richard**

O'Connell, Daniel
"the Liberator"

Campaigner for an independent Irish parliament

1775-1847

In 1800, the British Parliament passed an 'Act of Union'. This abolished the Irish Parliament. Instead, one hundred Irish members were to sit in the British Parliament along with Scottish, English and Welsh members. But most Irish people were Catholics*, and, until 1829, Catholics of any kind weren't allowed to sit in Parliament - fear of Catholics still ran deep. Irish Catholics naturally resented the new arrangement.

It was Daniel O'Connell's mission in life to get the Act of Union repealed. He campaigned both inside and outside Parliament. The campaign reached a peak in 1843 with 'Monster Meetings' throughout Ireland. At the largest, in August on the Hill of Tara, a *million* people came. Rebellion was in the air. O'Connell was arrested later in the year but released in 1844.

Then followed the terrible Irish Potato Famine (started 1845). The people started to turn to new leaders and O'Connell's star faded.

O'Donnell, Hugh Roe, Lord of Tyrconnel
" Red Hugh "

Irish Rebel who tackled the Tudors
around **1572-1602**

An old prophecy in Tyrconnel said that if one Lord Hugh succeeded another then all foreigners would be driven from the land. Well, Hugh O'Donnell was a Hugh and so was his father. Maybe the time had come.

The 'foreigner' was England. Protestant* England under **Elizabeth I** was fighting for its life against Catholic* Spain - and Catholic Ireland was the back door to England. If the English could control Ireland they could keep the back door closed.

Red Hugh hated English rule. His men once killed everyone aged over fifteen in Connaught who couldn't speak Gaelic (the old Irish language). He helped fellow rebel (and Hugh) **Hugh O'Neill** lead an Irish army to victory at the Battle of Yellow Ford in Armagh (1598). Then in late 1601, a Spanish force landed at Kinsale in the south. Hugh and his men rushed forty miles in twenty-four hours to help them (despite the fact that Hugh's toes had been amputated due to frostbite in 1591). But the Irish and Spanish forces were badly beaten by an English army. Hugh O'Donnell sailed to Spain where he died shortly after, probably poisoned.

O'Neill, Hugh
"the Great Earl"

Irish rebel who missed his chance

around **1540-1616**

Hugh O'Neill could perhaps have been king of all Ireland if he'd played his cards right. He didn't. Supported by **Hugh O'Donnell** and other Catholic* Irish rebels, O'Neill smashed a Protestant* English army at the Battle of Yellow Ford in Armagh in 1598 and most of Ireland rose up in rebellion at the news. But O'Neill failed to seize the moment and to lead the rebels to victory. Instead, he dithered. In 1599, another large English force under the **Earl of Essex** landed at Dublin - and both men dithered.

Then in 1600, Essex was replaced by Lord Mountjoy and the dithering was over. When Spanish forces landed at Kinsale in the south in 1601 to help O'Neill's rebels, Mountjoy besieged the Spaniards and then routed O'Neill and his rebel army.

O'Neill submitted to the English in 1603, six days after the death of **Elizabeth I**. But he wasn't happy about it. In 1607, he and other northern chiefs together with their families set sail for Spain in the 'Flight of the Earls'. O'Neill died in Rome nine years later.

Oates, Titus

Unpleasant person who invented the 'Popish Plot'

1649-1705

In 1675, Titus Oates was appointed Chaplain to the Protestants* in the household of the Duke of Norfolk. The Duke was the most important Catholic* in England and Oates decided to spy on Catholics. He pretended to become a Catholic himself and spent time in Catholic colleges in France.

Back in London in 1678, he invented what became known as the 'Popish Plot'. He said that Catholics were planning to murder King **Charles II** and put Charles's Catholic brother James (the future **James II**) on the throne. In the witch hunt that followed, thirty-five Catholics were executed. Eventually Oates was found out. He was pilloried, flogged and imprisoned for life. However after the 'Glorious Revolution' of 1688 he was released and even given a government pension.

Offa

Saxon king who built a dyke

died 796, KING OF MERCIA

Offa was King of the middle Saxon kingdom of Mercia from 757-96. He was a fierce warrior and became 'Bretwalda', most powerful King in England - so powerful that he felt he could address the Emperor Charlemagne as an equal (not that Charlemagne liked it very much).

Offa pushed the boundary between England and Wales further into Wales, building a huge earthwork known as 'Offa's Dyke' for seventy miles along the border. Parts of it are still there. During his reign, Lichfield in Mercia became an archbishopric, the only time there's been any other Archbishop in England apart from the Archbishops of Canterbury and York.

Old Pretender   *see* Stuart, Prince James Edward

Oswald, Saint

Saxon king and Saxon saint

around 604-642, KING OF NORTHUMBRIA

Get ready for Saxon squabbles: when Oswald was a youth he was driven from the Saxon kingdom of Bernicia in north-east England by **Edwin** who killed Oswald's father, King Æthelfrith the Ferocious. Bernicia was swallowed up in a new kingdom called Northumbria. Meanwhile Oswald fled to the Monastery of Iona in Scotland and there became a Christian. Later, after Edwin was dead, Oswald returned to become king of Northumbria.

With the help of **Saint Aidan**, Oswald reintroduced Christianity to Northumbria. They founded a monastery on Lindisfarne (Holy Island). In 642 he was killed by **Penda**, the pagan King of Mercia (in the Midlands) at Oswestry. 'Oswestry' probably means 'Oswald's Tree' and got its name because Penda stuck Oswald's head, hands and arms on stakes near the battlefield. By that time, Oswald was thought of as a saint, due to his returning Christianity to Northumbria and other good deeds.

His head was finally buried at Lindisfarne - until it was dug up again in 875 and carried to Durham in the coffin of St Cuthbert, to avoid being stolen by the Vikings. As late as 1828 it was still there - with Cuthbert.

Owen, Robert

Manufacturer who meant well

1771-1858

Robert Owen was an early socialist*. The son of a Welsh saddler from Newtown, he grew rich in the Manchester cotton trade and in 1799 bought the industrial village of New Lanark near Glasgow with some partners. His partners just wanted to make money, but Owen wanted more. He improved the housing and the working conditions in the New Lanark cotton mills, he opened a shop and an infant school - the first proper infant school in Britain.

New Lanark was a big success. Important people took an interest. (A Russian archduke even offered to take two million British people back to Russia to start Russian New Lanarks!) Other 'Owenite' communities followed, in particular New Harmony in Indiana, USA (founded 1824). Unfortunately New Harmony *wasn't* a success. People argued and Owen lost a lot of money.

He lost his money - but not his ideals. He kept on campaigning for trade unions and factory reform. He was still campaigning a month before he died - in Newtown where he started out.

Pankhurst, Emmeline

Suffragette leader

1858-1928

Emmeline Pankhurst was a 'suffragette'. 'Suffrage' means the 'right to vote', and a 'suffragette' was a woman who fought for women's right to vote. Emmeline led the fight in Britain.

In 1889, she helped found the Women's Franchise League ('franchise' also means 'right to vote') and then in 1903, with her daughter Christabel and a few others, she founded the Women's Social and Political Union. There was just one problem - nobody listened to them. So from 1906 the suffragettes became more and more militant (meaning: they went on the warpath to get people to pay attention). They broke up meetings, they broke windows, they chained themselves to railings, they went on hunger strike in prison. Emmeline was in the thick of it. In 1913, she was imprisoned and released twelve times under the 'Cat and Mouse' Act which let hunger strikers out of prison just until they got well again.

When World War I started in 1914, the suffragettes called off their campaign - but they'd already won the argument. In 1918, women over thirty got a part vote and then in 1928, an act giving equal rights to men and women over twenty-one was finally passed. Emmeline died shortly after.

179

Parnell, Charles Stewart

Irish 'Home Rule' campaigner

1846-91

Charles Parnell believed that Ireland would never be happy until the Irish people were allowed to rule themselves without England poking its nose in. Parnell fought for 'Home Rule' - for a separate parliament in Dublin with power to rule Ireland as it saw fit. There had been no separate Irish parliament since 1800. Irish MPs sat in the Westminster Parliament in London.

In 1875, Parnell was elected to Westminster. From then on he used every trick in the book to win his case, making himself one of the most unpopular men in England. But he didn't care - so long as he got Home Rule. And he came within a whisker of success: in 1886 Prime Minister **Gladstone** put a Home Rule bill before Parliament but was outvoted.

100

Then in 1890, Parnell was found to have had a love affair with Kitty O'Shea, wife of another 'Home Ruler'. How shocking! His enemies were delighted and the scandal ruined his career. He died in Brighton five months after marrying Kitty.

Parr, Catherine *see* **Henry VIII**

Patrick, Saint

Christian missionary for a snake-free Ireland

5TH CENTURY

Patrick was born in what is now Wales during the final years of the Roman Empire, when barbarian raiders were at the gate. His father was Roman-British and a Christian. Christianity was then the official religion of the Roman Empire. When Patrick was sixteen, he was seized from his father's villa by Irish raiders and taken to Ireland where he was sold as a slave. After six years working as a herdsman, he escaped back to England.

But he couldn't rest. He returned to Ireland and set about converting the natives to Christianity. It was very dangerous work, but by the time he died, Ireland was on its way to being a Christian country. Legend has it that Patrick drove the snakes from Ireland (there aren't any, apart from pets and in zoos), and that he explained the Christian trinity of Father, Son and Holy Ghost with the help of the three-leafed shamrock, now the Irish national plant.

Peel, Sir Robert

Prime Minister who planned a police force

1788-1850

In 1834, Robert Peel became the first 'Conservative'* Prime Minister of Britain. Up to that time the Conservatives had just been known as 'Tories'*. It was Peel more than anyone who laid the foundations of the modern, mass-membership Conservative Party. But that's not what he's most famous for. In 1829 as Home Secretary he started the Metropolitan Police Force - 1000 men in blue to patrol the streets of London. Since that time the British police have been called 'Peelers' and then 'Bobbies' after him - among other names.

Peel was very clever and used to work sixteen hours a day. He was also proud. He once challenged the Irish leader **O'Connell** to a duel, travelling to Ostend to fight him (it was illegal in Britain). Fortunately O'Connell was arrested in London and so the duel never happened. Peel died after a fall from his horse while he was riding in London.

172

Penda

Saxon king who killed Christians

577-655, KING OF MERCIA

Penda was a Saxon king and a fierce warrior. Due to him the kingdom of Mercia in the Midlands became one of the great Saxon kingdoms.

He was a pagan*. That meant he preferred the old Saxon gods Thunor and Woden to the new-fangled religion called Christianity, which was spreading fast. He did his best to stem the tide, killing **Edwin**, the Christian king of Northumbria, in 632 and King (Saint) **Oswald**, also a Christian and also a king of Northumbria, in 642.

80
177

It was yet another Christian Northumbrian who finally got the better of him. In 651, King Oswy 'cut off the heathen head' of Penda after a mammoth two-day battle near modern Leeds. The ferocious old pagan was at least eighty at the time of his death. Not bad, considering that most Saxon kings didn't live beyond their twenties.

Penn, William

Founder of Pennsylvania

1644-1718

Being a Quaker*, William Penn refused to take his hat off in front of his superiors, not even in front of the King **Charles II**. Not that Charles minded, in fact he was a friend. And at least Penn didn't preach naked as earlier Quakers had sometimes done!

49

In 1681 Charles granted him a huge area of land on the west bank of the Delaware River in North America. Penn called it 'Pennsylvania' in memory of his father, Admiral Penn. The grant was partly meant to cancel out a large debt that Charles had owed the Admiral.

Penn wanted Pennsylvania (and the next-door state of Delaware) to be a refuge for Quakers and other persecuted groups. From the first there was religious freedom for all Christian sects and there was an elected council. It was a huge success. When Penn arrived in 1682 the capital Philadelphia (means 'brotherly love') was already being laid out. When he left for the last time in 1701, Pennsylvania was firmly established.

Pepys, Samuel
"Father of the navy"

Diarist of genius

1633-1703

Samuel Pepys is known as the 'Father of the Navy' because as head of the Admiralty his hard work turned the British navy into the strongest navy in the world. He was also president of the Royal Society*.

Which is all very amazing ... but what's *really* amazing about Pepys is that we can read about what he did, not only from the *outside* as others saw him - but also from the *inside*, as he saw himself. Starting in 1660 he wrote a diary. This diary, written in code and meant for his eyes alone, is one of the greatest works ever written in English. Through Pepys' eyes we can see seventeenth century London almost as if we were there, including accounts of the Great Plague and the Fire of London. He hides nothing, not even his own weaknesses.

He stopped writing in 1669 because his eyes were hurting and he thought he was going blind. It was almost, as he put it: 'as much as to see himself go into his grave'.

Percy, Sir Henry   *see* Hotspur

Pitt, William
"Pitt the Younger"

Prime Minister who nobbled Napoleon
1759-1806

William Pitt was Britain's youngest ever Prime Minister. He took on the job in 1783 when only twenty-four. He had a good start - he was the second son of **William Pitt the Elder**, also a Prime Minister. Rather a lonely man, Pitt the Younger's only real vice was port wine, which he started drinking for his health on the questionable advice of a doctor.

Pitt resigned in 1801 because King **George III** refused to agree to give the vote to Roman Catholics*, but he bounced back three years later when Britain came under threat of invasion by French revolutionary armies under Napoleon. He led Britain during the first half of the Napoleonic War.

Pitt, the 'Saviour of Europe', died ten years before Napoleon was finally defeated, worn out by hard work - and too much port wine.

Pitt, William, 'The Elder' *see* **Chatham**

Pole, Reginald, Cardinal
"Cardinal Pole"

Catholic cardinal who helped Bloody Mary

1500-58

120 Cardinal Pole was **Henry VIII's** cousin. He was also a Catholic* and believed that the Pope should be the head of all Christian Churches. So when Henry turned the church *in* England into the Church *of* England with himself, Henry, at its head, Pole didn't agree with him - which was a dangerous thing to do. From 1532, Pole lived in Italy. Henry meanwhile executed Pole's brother and mother.

79 Years passed and Henry was succeeded by **Edward VI** who didn't like Catholics either. It was only in 1554 after
150 Catholic **Mary** came to the throne that it was safe for Pole to return. Mary meant to turn Protestant* England back into a Catholic country. She asked Pole to help her. Many Protestants were burned during her short
59 unhappy reign, including Archbishop **Cranmer** (1556). Pole replaced him.

It didn't last long. In 1557 the Pope (of all people) unfairly accused Pole of heresy, which was a serious charge. Then Mary died. Poor Archbishop Pole, dead upset, died twelve hours later.

Pope, Alexander

Tiny man - big poet

1688-1744

When he was a boy, Alexander Pope was whipped for 'satirizing' his teacher. Satirizing people, that is making fun of them, was something Pope was very good at. He needed some way of standing up for himself because, due to a childhood illness, he never grew taller than 1.36 metres (4 ft 6 in) and he was so weak that in middle age he had to wear a stiff canvas bodice just to help him stay upright. He was also a Catholic* and therefore not allowed to stand for Parliament or go to university. Words were his only weapons and he made full use of them - which is not to say that he only used them to make fun of people.

Pope became the greatest poet of his age. Among his most famous poems are: *The Dunciad*, *The Rape of the Lock* and *An Essay on Man*. He liked to write in beautiful two-line rhymes known as 'heroic couplets'. Their beauty came from hard work as well as from talent. As he said:

True ease in writing comes from art, not chance,
As those move easiest who have learned to dance.

Bear that in mind if you like writing poetry.

Priestley, Joseph

Scientist who fathered the fizzy drink and 'discovered' oxygen

1733-1804

Joseph Priestley was the first person to call rubber 'rubber' - because it rubs things out. More importantly he 'discovered' several gases. In 1767, while he was living next door to a Leeds brewery, he became interested in the little bubbles of gas given off as beer ferments. He discovered that this gas (carbon dioxide), then known as 'fixed air', could be dissolved in water to make a pleasant drink, now called 'soda water'. Other experiments followed. In all, Priestley discovered ten gases, including oxygen, for which he's most famous (actually a Swedish chemist, Wilhelm Scheele, discovered oxygen a year before he did, and it was a French scientist, Lavoisier, who called it oxygen).

Priestley, a Christian minister, was *against* the slave trade and *for* the French Revolution. In 1791, an anti-revolutionary mob burned down his house in Birmingham. He left for America in 1794 and never returned to Britain.

Princes in the Tower *see* Edward V & Richard III

Purcell, Henry

Superb songwriter

around 1658-1695

Henry Purcell's father died when Purcell was five and he was adopted by his uncle Thomas, a court musician under **Charles II**. By the age of six, little Henry was a choirboy of the Chapel Royal. By fourteen he'd probably started composing. From then until his death at the young age of thirty-seven, music poured from his pen like water from a well. He's specially famous for many beautiful songs and for his first opera, *Dido and Aeneas*, which was written for a Chelsea girls' school.

49

Raleigh, Sir Walter
"the Last of the Tudors"

Tudor courtier, poet and adventurer

around 1554-1618

Walter Raleigh was one of **Elizabeth I's** favourite courtiers. He was a handsome man with dark brown hair and a strong Devon accent. (Elizabeth's nickname

85

for him was 'Water' because of the way he said 'Walter'.) He was a poet and a fearless soldier. As the main organizer of the new colony of Virginia in America, which he started in 1584, he introduced the potato and tobacco into England. He himself smoked a pipe and it's said that he even persuaded Elizabeth to have a puff.

Elizabeth didn't like her courtiers to fall in love with anyone except her. Sir Walter lost her friendship after he fell for the beautiful Elizabeth Throckmorton in 1592, whom he later married. Then in 1603 the old queen died and the new king, **James I**, accused him of conspiracy. Sir Walter was locked in the Tower of London for fifteen years - until 1618, when he was released one last time to head an expedition to South America in quest of gold, and perhaps of the legendary city of gold, Eldorado.

The expedition failed and on his return Walter Raleigh was beheaded.

Reynolds, Sir Joshua

Pleasant portrait painter

1723-92

When he was a young man, Joshua Reynolds became partly deaf due to a 'cold' caught while painting in Rome. Perhaps the deafness helped him to *look* more clearly than most people. Back in London he became the top portrait painter of his time. He painted dukes by the dozen, loads of ladies and cart-loads of gentlemen. Some of his best paintings were portraits of children, such as *Master Crewe as Henry VIII*. Unfortunately, many of his paintings aren't looking too good any more: the flesh colours have faded to a ghostly white.

Reynolds was fun to be with. He was always out at parties and dinners. He helped found the 'Literary Club' (dinner every Monday in the Turk's Head) so that 134 his good friend **Samuel Johnson** would have 'unlimited opportunities for talking'. In 1768, he became the first President of the Royal Academy.

Rhodes, Cecil John

Victorian empire builder

1853-1902

As a young man Cecil Rhodes got very, very rich by mining for diamonds in South Africa. By 1890, his De Beers Consolidated Mines Co. Ltd controlled most world diamond production.

That was just the beginning. Rhodes believed that the British Empire was a very good thing and he wanted to make it even bigger and better. He dreamed of a huge federation of British controlled states covering the whole southern quarter of Africa. By 1890 he was Prime Minister of Cape Colony (part of what is now South Africa) and used this position to further his plans. He had set up the British South African Co. (chartered 1889) and the vast territories of this company, gained by hook or by crook from native African rulers, became an entirely new country, then called *Rhodesia*. Native Africans have at last won back control of this area which is now divided into the two modern countries, Zambia and Zimbabwe.

Richard I
"the Lionheart"

Crusader king who fought away

1157-99, King of England (Plantagenet)

115 Richard was the third son of **Henry II** and a mighty warrior. In 1189, he rebelled against his father, hounded him to death and became king.

He never spent a full year in England. The Muslims under their dashing leader Saladin had captured Jerusalem in 1187 and in 1190 Richard set off on the Third Crusade* to win it back. He was the richest and most warlike of all the crusaders. In 1191 they captured Acre and Richard slaughtered 2700 Muslim prisoners outside the walls, within sight of the enemy, because their ransoms were unpaid. On his way back from the crusade he was shipwrecked, then made his way through Europe in disguise until he was captured by his enemies in Vienna. The huge sum paid to the German Emperor for his release (150,000 marks) shows that England was already a very rich country.

132 Back home in England (1194) he forgave his brother **John** who'd tried to steal the kingdom, then spent the rest of his life in France - fighting. He died while besieging a castle in Normandy.

Richard II

Mediocre medieval monarch

1367-1400, KING OF ENGLAND (PLANTAGENET)

Legend said that Richard II, grandson and successor of
77 **Edward III**, was born without a skin. If true this would
have been bad news, because he needed a thick one.
Richard wasn't cut out for kingship and his reign ended
in disaster.

He became king in 1377 when he was only ten and for
133 twelve years the country was ruled for him by **John of
Gaunt**, Duke of Lancaster. During that time Richard's
courage helped put down the Peasants' Revolt (1381).
From 1389 he ruled personally. The first eight years
went well, but then he turned nasty and executed some
powerful nobles. In 1399, John of Gaunt's son, the
116 future **Henry IV**, led a rebellion against him. Richard
was forced to hand over his crown and was probably
starved to death in Pontefract Castle the following year.

Richard III

Monarch - and multiple murderer?

1452-85 KING OF ENGLAND (HOUSE OF YORK)

Richard III was the last King of England to rule during the Wars of the Roses* (1455-85), fought between followers of the red rose of York and the white rose of Lancaster. He was the younger brother of the Yorkist
78 king **Edward IV** and served him well, probably helping
118 out in the murder of **Henry VI** in 1471. When Edward died in 1483, Richard became protector of Edward's
78 twelve-year-old son, **Edward V**. Within weeks, he locked young Edward and his brother in the Tower of London and had himself crowned king. Soon after that, the two little 'Princes in the Tower' disappeared - probably murdered on Richard's orders.

With so many murders behind him, it's hardly surprising that Richard was made the evil villain of
198 **Shakespeare's** play *Richard III*. But there's another reason: Shakepeare lived in the days of the Tudors and the Tudors were Richard's enemies. In 1485, Henry Tudor landed in Wales determined to force Richard from the throne. He defeated Richard at the Battle of Bosworth, south of Leicester. Richard died fighting and
119 Henry Tudor then became **Henry VII**, the first Tudor king of England, thus ending the Wars of the Roses.

Robin Hood

Outlaw who dressed in green

date unknown

Robin Hood is probably only a legend, although he may just possibly be real, based on a medieval outlaw from South Yorkshire, near Barnsley. Some later stories place Robin in the reign of **Richard I**, and certainly by 1300 Robin was a popular hero. Common people loved the idea of an outlaw who lived free in the forest and robbed the rich to give to the poor and outwitted evil villains such as the Sheriff of Nottingham. His stories were later acted at May Day festivals; in fact May Day was sometimes known as 'Robin Hood Day'. There are rocks, hills and wells called after him all over England.

Ruskin, John

Victorian art critic and writer

1819-1900

During the nineteenth century, Britain went through a revolution - the Industrial Revolution. Huge cities such as Manchester and Birmingham sprang up where before there'd been only country towns. Many artists and designers longed for the beauty of nature or looked back to a time before this revolution, to the Middle

Ages. That's why so many Victorian buildings are built in the 'Gothic' style of medieval churches and why early nineteenth century poets such as **Wordsworth** chose to live in out-of-the-way places such as the Lake District.

242

Ruskin was the champion of the gothic style, of 'medieval-style' painters such as the Pre-Raphaelites and of Romantic nature poets and artists such as Wordsworth and **Turner**. His books *Modern Painters*, *The Seven Lamps of Architecture* and *The Stones of Venice* were read by thousands and by the time he died his words were treated with great respect by artists and fellow critics alike.

219

Seymour, Jane *see* **Henry VIII**

Shakespeare, William

Mysterious Tudor playwright
1564-1616

William Shakespeare was born in Stratford-on-Avon. When he was eighteen he married twenty-six-year-old Anne Hathaway who was pregnant and they had twins. His life is a bit of a mystery, but it's known that by 1592 he'd moved to London and had become a successful actor and playwright. His plays were the talk of Tudor London and were acted before **Elizabeth I**. He made money and was part-owner of the famous Globe Theatre, now rebuilt.

85

In middle age he returned to Stratford where he seems to have lived the life of a comfortable gentleman. When he died he left his 'second best bed' to his wife Anne, and to the world he left many of the greatest plays ever written.

Shaw, George Bernard

Socialist playwright who wrote the original of *My Fair Lady*

1856-1950

George Bernard Shaw was a vegetarian socialist* with a big, bristly beard and a sense of humour. As a young man he was shy, but he turned himself into a brilliant public speaker by practising in parks. He used his talent to help the cause of socialism.

Shaw wrote some of the best plays of modern times, such as *Man and Superman*, and *Saint Joan* (about the French heroine Joan of Arc). His play *Pygmalion* was made into the famous musical *My Fair Lady*.

Shelley, Percy Bysshe

Passionate poet

1792-1822

Percy Bysshe Shelley believed in freedom and poetry. In 1814 he ran away with Harriet, the sixteen-year-old daughter of a London hotel keeper. The young couple moved from place to place. In Dublin Shelley called for Irish freedom and in North Wales he launched toy boats into the sea calling for freedom everywhere.

By 1816 he'd separated from Harriet and was in Geneva with Mary Godwin, daughter of **Mary Wollstonecraft**. (Mary was writing her famous novel *Frankenstein*.) Harriet meanwhile drowned herself in the Serpentine (she'd threatened suicide earlier). Shelley married Mary (1818) and soon they were in Italy with **Lord Byron**. Four years later Shelley was dead, drowned in a storm off the Italian coast. His body was burned on the Italian shore. A friend thrust his hand into the flames and removed the heart, which was taken back to England in a box.

Shelley wrote fierce political poems such as *The Mask of Anarchy*, beautiful love poems such as *To Jane the Invitation* and other passionate poems such as *Ode to the West Wind* and *Ode to a Skylark*.

Sidney, Sir Philip

Perfect Tudor gentleman

1554-86

Sir Philip Sidney was what all gentlemen are meant to be and very few are: he was noble, kind, brave and generous. He was also a poet. His sonnet (a type of poem) sequence *Astrophel and Stella* was a breakthrough for English poetry.

85 Sidney shone like a star at the court of **Elizabeth I**. When in 1585 she decided to help the Protestant* Dutch against their Catholic* Spanish overlords, Sidney was made governor of the Dutch town of Flushing. The following September, Sidney joined an attack on a Spanish force near Zütphen. The English were outnumbered six to one but Sidney charged three times through the enemy lines until a Spanish bullet pierced his thigh. Back in camp he asked for a bottle of water and was about to drink it when he saw a wounded soldier. He handed over the bottle with the famous words, 'Thy necessity is greater than mine'.

Sir Philip died within three weeks from an infection in his wound.

Simnel, Lambert

Fake royal

around 1475-1535

119 When **Henry VII** became the first Tudor King of England in 1485, his enemies from the old royal family of York wanted to remove him from the throne. Young Lambert Simnel, the son of a baker, was trained to pretend to be one of the Princes in the Tower (see

196, 78, **Richard III & Edward V**), the murdered sons of

78 **Edward IV**, and therefore the 'rightful' Yorkist heir to the throne. Later he pretended to be the son of Edward IV's brother, the Duke of Clarence. Lambert was crowned 'Edward VI' in Dublin. He was defeated by Henry's forces at the Battle of Stoke in 1487. Henry was merciful - young Lambert was allowed to live and was given a job in the royal kitchens.

Simpson, Mrs Wallis   *see* Edward VIII

Simpson, Sir James Young

Doctor who first used chloroform

1811-70

James Simpson was a Scottish doctor. In 1846 he heard how young American doctors and dentists had started giving ether to their patients. The ether was an *anaesthetic* - it made the patients go unconscious. This was a fantastic advance. Up to that time just about the only way to dull the pain of an operation was to make the patient blind drunk.

Simpson experimented with ether but found that it was far from perfect. He looked for something else which would do the trick. In 1847, with two assistants, he tried breathing chloroform. Next thing they knew they were underneath the table - they'd found the answer. Soon chloroform was being used successfully by doctors all over the world.

Actually choloroform can be *more* dangerous than ether, but for the time being it was just what patients needed. Simpson became Queen **Victoria's** official doctor and was made a baronet for his services to medicine.

Smith, Adam

Thinker about money

1723-90

Adam Smith was a Scottish professor. In 1776 he published his famous book: *Inquiry into the Nature and Causes of the Wealth of Nations*. The book sets out to uncover what makes some countries get rich.

Very broadly, Smith thought that two forces are at war within us: on the one hand greed and selfishness and on the other hand 'sympathy' and reason. It's the greed which produces wealth, making people *compete* with each other to make and sell things. Free *competition* leads to greater riches all round. But left to itself this greed can also lead to *monopoly* where the successful or powerful have too much power and can stop the competition. As Smith put it: 'the mean rapacity [greed], the monopoly spirit, of merchants or manufacturers, who neither are nor ought to be the rulers of mankind.'

Tell that to your local supermarket next time you go there!

Speke, John Hanning

Victorian explorer who 'discovered' the source of the Nile

1827-64

In 1856, the Royal Geographical Society sent John Speke
34 on an expedition to East Africa lead by **Richard Burton**.
Their aim was to discover the whereabouts of a large
lake then known as 'Nyasa', which was said to lie to the
east of what is now Kenya and which might be the
source of the River Nile. Speke and Burton explored
Lake Tanganyika and then Burton, who was sick,
agreed that Speke should go on alone to explore
another, larger lake to the north. Thus it was that Speke
became the first European to see Lake Victoria which he
223 called after Queen **Victoria**.

In 1860 Speke returned to Lake Victoria. At the end of
this expedition, again on his own, he saw where the
Nile flows out of the lake to the north. However, back in
Britain, Burton couldn't accept that Speke had
discovered the source of the Nile. A public debate
between them was arranged for 18th September 1864.
Unfortunately, on the morning of the debate, Speke
accidentally shot himself while out shooting partridge.

Stanhope, Lady Hester Lucy

Lady traveller and animal lover

1776-1839

From 1803-6 Lady Stanhope looked after the household of her uncle **William Pitt the Younger**. She was wild even then, and once blackened his face with burnt cork.

After he died, she didn't care for life in Britain any longer. In 1810 she set off for the East. After a brief spell in Jerusalem and then lording it over a large Arab camp, she settled in a ruined monastery on the slopes of Mount Lebanon. There she lived with at least thirty slaves and servants and a large army of cats, dogs and other animals. She poked her nose into local politics and many locals half-worshipped her as a sort of prophetess. What she liked doing best, however, was telling her European visitors what was wrong with Britain. Ideally she would talk until two or three in the morning. Her poor visitor would have to stand while she herself lay on a couch with a pipe in her mouth.

In August 1838, she shut herself up in her 'castle' and stayed there alone except for five servants until she died the following June.

Stanley, Sir Henry Morton

Victorian voyager to darkest Africa

1841-1904

John Rowlands was a poor Welsh boy. In 1859 he left Wales for New Orleans and there was befriended by a merchant called Henry Stanley. Ashamed of his poor background, John Rowland changed his name to 'Henry Morton Stanley'. After a few years the man with the new name got a job as reporter on the *New York Herald Tribune*. In 1871, he was told to go find the famous explorer **David Livingstone**, who'd disappeared in Africa, and to bring him back.

Stanley found Livingstone at Ujiji on the shores of Lake Tanganyika, greeting him with the famous words: 'Dr Livingstone, I presume.' The two men became friends and explored the north of the Lake together. Livingstone stayed on to die. Stanley returned to Britain to fame and fortune.

More was to follow. From 1874-7 in an epic three-year journey he traced the mighty Congo River from its source in East Africa right across to the Atlantic Ocean. In 1879, he returned yet again to found the Congo Free State for the King of Belgium. And in 1886 for his last adventure, he started at the mouth of the Congo, travelling from west to east on a mission to the Sudan to rescue Emin Pasha, a British ally.

Stephen

King caught in a civil war

around 1097-1154, KING OF ENGLAND (NORMAN)

'A mild man, soft and good, he did no justice' - that's how Stephen was described by a medieval writer, meaning that he was a nice enough man but not a very good king.

114 Medieval muddle now follows: when his uncle **Henry I** died in 1135, Stephen seized the crown of England, backed by most of the English nobles. Henry had meant
153 his own daughter **Matilda** to be queen, but the nobles wouldn't let a woman rule over them. Matilda landed from France in 1139 to fight for her rights, and civil war raged (on and off) until Matilda left again (1148). However, Stephen had made many enemies and the country was in a mess. When Matilda's son Henry of
115 Anjou, the future **Henry II**, landed from France (1153), Stephen was forced to agree that Henry would be the next king. In the meantime, Henry would rule the country as Stephen's adopted son. Stephen died one year later.

Stephenson, George

Inventor who built the first useful steam train

1781-1848

On 27 September 1825, the world's first passenger train service opened for business on the Stockton to Darlington railway line. George Stephenson was the engineer. His engine, the Active, pulled 450 passengers in 38 carriages at 15 mph (24 kph). For the first time ever passengers were able to travel faster than a galloping horse. Stephenson's train ran on 'flanged' wheels (common to all modern trains).

The next year, he became engineer to a new railway planned to run between Liverpool and Manchester. His new train, the Rocket, was a great improvement on the earlier version. It could travel at up to 36 mph (58 kph).

People weren't used to these sorts of speeds. At the grand opening on 15 September 1830, the MP William Huskisson was run over and later died. The world's first railway accident had also arrived.

Stevenson, Robert Louis

Children's adventure writer

1850-94

Robert Louis Stevenson sailed to the South Seas in 1888. By then he was a wealthy and world famous writer. He spent his last five years on the Pacific island of Samoa, where he was known as Tusitala, 'Teller of Tales', by the Samoans. They buried him on the remote summit of Mount Vaea. It took sixty men to cut a path through the jungle to his grave site.

Mount Vaea was a long way from the streets of Edinburgh where he started life, the son of a Scottish civil engineer. Fame had only come in 1883 when his children's adventure story, *Treasure Island* was published, but from then on there'd been a string of bestsellers. Among other wonderful books he wrote *A Child's Garden of Verses* (1885) *Kidnapped* (1886), *The Strange Case of Dr. Jekyll and Mr Hyde* (1886). They're still very good to read today.

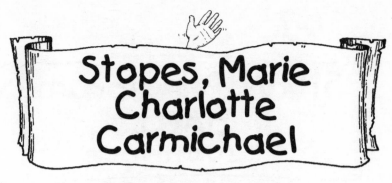

Stopes, Marie Charlotte Carmichael

Birth control pioneer

1880-1958

In the old days a married woman would normally give birth to a new baby every couple of years. Ten children in a family was quite common. This was exhausting for the mothers who often died young. Marie Stopes saw that by using birth control women could live longer and happier lives. Her books *Married Love* (1918) and *Wise Parenthood* (1918) sold in huge numbers around the world. In 1921 she opened the Mothers' Clinic for Birth Control in Holloway, London in 1921. It was the first ever birth control clinic of its kind in Britain.

Without the work of pioneers like Marie Stopes, many women would still have armfuls of babies to take care of - whether they want to or not.

Stuart, Prince James Edward
"the Old Pretender"

Catholic king that never was
1688-1766

On 10 June 1688 a baby was born in St James' Palace London, the only son of **James II**. 'How very convenient for the king,' people thought, believing that James, a Catholic*, wanted a Catholic son and heir to help turn Britain into a Catholic country. They said that the baby had been smuggled into the queen's bed in a warming pan.

By December James and his baby son had been driven out of the country in the 'Glorious Revolution' which saw Protestant* **William III** come to the throne. The baby boy grew up to become 'The Old Pretender' to the British throne. He tried to win the crown several times but died a disappointed man in Rome.

Swift, Jonathan
"Dean Swift"

The man who wrote *Gulliver's Travels*

1667-1745

Jonathan Swift had a wicked sense of humour. He used it to fight for common sense as he saw it, to defend what he felt was safe and reasonable in politics or religion. 'We have just enough religion to make us hate, but not enough to make us love one another', he once wrote.

Among his greatest works are *A Tale of a Tub* (published 1704), *Gulliver's Travels* (1726) and *A Modest Proposal* (1729) - in which he suggests that poor Irish children should be served as delicacies on the tables of the rich to solve the Irish population problem!

He was brought up in Dublin and returned there in 1714 to spend the rest of his life as the Dean of Saint Patrick's Cathedral. In later years his mind started to go. In fact he'd guessed that this might happen: he's supposed to have said: 'I shall be like that tree, I shall die at the top'.

Talbot, William Henry Fox

Pioneer of photography

1800-77

In 1839, Fox Talbot announced his invention of 'photogenic drawing', a method of making photographic prints on paper treated with silver chloride. A few weeks earlier and he would now be known as the inventor of photography instead of the Frenchman, Louis Daguerre, who'd just announced his own invention of the 'daguerrotype'. However, Fox Talbot's book *The Pencil of Nature* was the first book to be illustrated with photographs.

Fox Talbot went on to invent the first system of photographic negatives (1841) and a type of flash photography (1851). Modern photographic techniques developed out of his inventions rather than those of his rival Daguerre.

Tallis, Thomas

around 1510-1585, COMPOSER

Thomas Tallis was one of the great early composers of English music. He became a gentleman of the royal chapel around 1540 and was a friend of **William Byrd**.

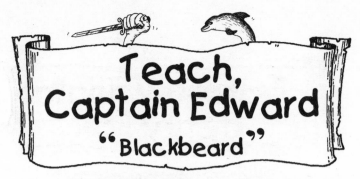

Teach, Captain Edward "Blackbeard"

Terrifying pirate chief

died 1718

In 1713 at the end of the War of Spanish Succession (1701-14), many English sailors refused to stop fighting. They stayed on in the West Indies as pirates, where they preyed on French and Spanish shipping. Worst of the lot was Edward Teach, or 'Blackbeard' as he was known due to his large, bristly beard. He was a huge, violent man. He used to light candles round his hat so as to make himself look frightening and he drank gunpowder with his rum.

The Royal Navy caught up with him in a narrow creek in North Carolina. Blackbeard was shot dead, then his head was chopped off and tied to the bowsprit of his ship. Legend says that he buried his treasure on London Island, off the coast of New England, leaving wife number fourteen to guard it. She died in 1753 - but her ghost guards it still.

Telford, Thomas

Bridge builder and engineer

1757-1834

In April 1825, some friends of Thomas Telford came to congratulate him on raising the first of the sixteen massive 23.75 ton chains of the Menai Suspension bridge. They found him praying with relief. The Menai Bridge was his greatest work and he hadn't slept for weeks from worrying.

Even if it *had* fallen down, he had plenty of other projects to be proud of: more than 900 miles (1,450km) of Scottish roads, 1200 Scottish bridges, the main road from Chester to Holyhead (now the A5), the St Katherine's Docks in London and many more. All this by the son of a Scottish shepherd, who as a cheerful boy, known as 'Laughing Tam', had herded cattle for the farmers near his mother's cottage.

Tennyson, Alfred, 1st Baron
(Lord Alfred Tennyson)

Very Victorian poet

1809-92

Alfred Tennyson's most famous poems include: *In Memoriam*, *Lady of Shalott* and *Morte d'Arthur*. They are often set in medieval times. In later life Tennyson became addicted to port and tobacco and his poems became rather stuffy and prudish - which is hardly surprising since he was the top poet of the Victorian age, which is famous for being stuffy and prudish. Queen **Victoria** loved his work and made him Poet Laureate on the death of **William Wordsworth** in 1850. (The Poet Laureate is the official poet to the king or queen.)

223
242

Tone, (Theobald) Wolfe

Irish freedom fighter

1763-98

Wolfe Tone believed that Protestant* and Catholic* Irishmen should unite to fight for freedom from British rule. In 1791 he founded the Society of United Irishmen to start the struggle. It was mainly Protestant but believed in equal rights for Catholics.

By 1796 shock waves from the French Revolution of 1789 had spread across Europe. Tone hoped that the French would help Irish revolutionaries like himself. He persuaded the French government to send an army of 14,000 men to Ireland and sailed with it as Adjutant-General. They were driven back by a fearful storm.

He tried again with a smaller French force in 1798, but a British naval squadron caught up with them off the Irish coast. Tone was taken to Dublin to be tried as a traitor. He cut his throat with a penknife on the eve of his execution.

Townshend, Charles, 2nd Viscount
" Turnip Townshend "

Farming fanatic and politician

1674-1738

Viscount Townshend was a leading figure in the government of **George I**, together with his brother-in-law **Robert Walpole**. He resigned in 1730 and retired to his estate in Norfolk. There he set out to improve local methods of farming.

95
225

If the same crop is grown year after year in the same soil, the soil becomes poorer and poorer. Townshend 'rotated' his crops - sowing different crops in different years. He experimented with clover which adds nitrogen to the soil, and with the turnips which gave him his nickname. Turnips made good cattle fodder, cattle made good manure, and the manure could be put back on the land to enrich it further.

Turner, Joseph Mallord William

Artist who painted light

1775-1851

William Turner was one of the greatest British painters. His paintings were light years ahead of their time - with the accent on *light*. They just glowed with it. Some people thought they were wishy-washy, but they weren't. In fact, they were the result of a lifetime of hard work - during just one trip to Italy in 1819 he made 1500 drawings. He left 19,000 drawings to the National Gallery as well as a huge number of paintings.

Turner was very shy and this made him rude and cranky. He was also secretive and tight with money. In fact he was so secretive that from 1839 he had a secret second house in Chelsea where he lived part-time as 'Mr Booth', the name of his housekeeper. In 1851 when he died, local people must have been surprised to discover that 'Puggy Booth' as they knew him was actually the famous William Turner, soon to be buried in St Paul's Cathedral.

Turpin, Dick

Hard-hearted highwayman
1705-39

Dick Turpin was an Essex butcher's apprentice. He took up cattle stealing then joined a gang of robbers. They picked on lonely Essex farmhouses, tortured the inhabitants and stole their money. When the ringleaders were arrested, Turpin got away and took up with a famous highwayman called Tom King. Unfortunately (for King) Turpin shot King while trying to shoot a policeman.

Turpin escaped to Yorkshire and for a while lived as a horse dealer under his mother's name, Palmer. But in 1739 he was arrested for horse stealing and sentenced to death. Before he was hanged, he confessed to a murder and several horrible burglaries.

Tyler, Wat (Walter Tyler)

Leader of the Peasants' Revolt

died 1381

In May 1381, English peasants rose up in the Peasants' Revolt sparked off by a new, unpopular poll tax. The men of Kent chose Wat to be their captain. They captured Canterbury then marched on London, firing the Savoy Palace of the unpopular noble **John of Gaunt** on 13 June. Next day, while the young King **Richard II** was talking with peasant rebels from Essex, the men of Kent captured the Tower of London and executed the Archbishop of Canterbury.

133
195

On 15 June Richard met the rebels again, at Smithfield then just outside London. By now Wat was leader of the entire rebellion. Among other things, he demanded that church lands should be given to villagers. A fight broke out and Wat was wounded by the Lord Mayor of London. His supporters carried him bleeding to St. Bartholomew's Hospital but he was dragged out and beheaded shortly after by the Lord Mayor's men. The Peasants' Revolt ended with him.

Tyndale, William

Translator of the Bible - he staked his life on it

around 1492-1536

William Tyndale was a Protestant*. He believed that the rich, priest-ridden Catholic* church of his time needed to be reformed lock, stock and barrel. A brilliant scholar of ancient Greek, Latin and Hebrew, he decided to translate the Bible into English so that people would have the chance to read it for themselves. Before then only Latin versions had been available. From 1524 he worked on his translation in the safety of Protestant Germany. When his New Testament came out in 1525 it was a huge success.

Tyndale never finished translating the Bible. In 1536 he was captured by Catholic agents in Antwerp and given over to the power of the Catholic German Emperor. He was burned at the stake, having first been strangled. But they couldn't burn his words. His strong, simple language has influenced English writing from that day to this.

Victoria

Long-lived queen who dressed in black

1819-1901, QUEEN OF GREAT BRITAIN AND IRELAND AND EMPRESS OF INDIA (HOUSE OF HANOVER)

Queen Victoria ruled Britain for sixty-four years, almost the entire time that Britain was a world super-power. When she came to the throne in 1837, she was a lively young woman of eighteen who liked dancing and ball-gowns. When she died she was a very fat, old woman who always dressed in black. She'd started wearing black after she lost her husband Prince Albert in 1861. They'd been happy for twenty-one years and had had nine children. In her grief she hid herself away and avoided appearing in public for years. She became known as the 'Royal Malingerer'.

69 In 1876 Prime Minister **Disraeli** arranged for her to be declared 'Empress of India' (part of the British Empire at that time). Gradually she came out of hiding and in 1887, when she'd been Queen for fifty years, she held a Golden Jubilee. Millions from all over the world joined in the celebrations. By the end of her life she was even more popular than at the beginning.

Vortigern
"Haughty Tyrant"

British ruler who let in the Saxons

active 425-450

Vortigern (meaning 'Supreme Leader') seems to have ruled a large chunk of Britain during the dark years after the fall of the Roman Empire. The Romans had withdrawn their legions in 409 and Britain was under attack from barbarian raiders on all sides. Vortigern decided to fight fire with fire. He invited a party of barbarian Saxons under their leaders **Hengist** and Horsa to help him fight off the barbarian Scots and Picts from the north. The Saxons landed in Kent. They helped defeat the Scots and Picts but then they turned on their British hosts and routed them too, in four bloody battles. This was the start of the Saxon invasion of Britain - and the beginning of the end for the ancient British.

113

Wallace, Sir William

Scottish hero

around 1270-1305

75 Mighty **Edward I**, Hammer of the Scots, seized power in Scotland in 1296, removing the Scottish king John de

Balliol. He then disappeared to France to fight the French. That's when rebel leader William Wallace led a Scottish fight-back against English rule. He routed an English army at the Battle of Stirling Bridge (1297) and was then declared 'Guardian' of Scotland, ruling for the absent John de Balliol.

But by 1298, Edward was back. He marched into Scotland at the head of a large army and smashed Wallace's forces near Falkirk. Wallace fought on for a while but he was captured in 1305 and taken to London. There he was tried in Westminster Hall, with a crown of laurel leaves on his head to mock him for having dared to rule Scotland. He was executed as a traitor.

Walpole, Sir Robert, Earl of Orford

First British prime minister

1676-1745

Robert Walpole was officially Lord of the Treasury and Chancellor of the Exchequer - *not* prime minister. There weren't any prime ministers in those days, in fact he hated the expression. But prime minister is what he was really in all but name from 1721-42 - the very first Prime Minister of Britain. He was given Number 10 Downing Street which has been the official home of British prime ministers ever since.

95 Walpole rose to power during the reign of **George I** who was German and couldn't speak English. George thought Parliament was boring and was happy to leave the running of the Government to Walpole, who was brilliant and a very crafty politician (he hid his craftiness beneath an honest, friendly manner). By the

96 time **George II** came to the throne in 1727, Walpole was so good at his job that George II also supported him in power. Walpole's fall from government after twenty-one years at the top was mainly due to old age - which is more than can be said for most of the prime ministers who came after him.

Walsingham, Sir Francis

Tudor spy chief

around **1532-1590**

85 In 1573 Francis Walsingham joined **Elizabeth I's** government. At that time Protestant* England was under threat from Catholic* Spain, the most powerful country in the world. Walsingham realized that

Elizabeth had to know what the Catholics were up to, so as to foil Catholic plans for invasion or rebellion. His favourite saying was: 'Knowledge is never bought too dear.' At one time he had fifty-three agents in foreign courts and another eighteen spies on other secret business. Due to his work, Elizabeth was able to foil deadly Catholic plots such as the Babington Plot (1586) ¹⁵¹ which led to the trial and execution of **Mary Queen of Scots**, and to have advance warning of the Spanish invasion fleet known as the Armada (1588).

Walsingham never made much money from his job. Elizabeth doesn't seem to have liked him very much, perhaps because he favoured the extreme Protestants known as Puritans*. He died poor and in debt.

Warbeck, Perkin

Fake royal

around 1474-1499

¹¹⁹ When **Henry VII** became the first Tudor King of England in 1485, he had many enemies among the old kingly family of York which he'd just defeated. Perkin Warbeck pretended to be Richard Duke of York, the ¹⁹⁶ younger of the two Princes in the Tower (see **Richard III** ⁷⁸ and **Edward V**). As Duke of York he could claim to be

the rightful Yorkist king of England. (The same sort of trick had been tried four years earlier by **Lambert Simnel**.) Perkin convinced many important people that he was royal. He even married a cousin of **James IV**, King of Scotland.

Perkin was captured in Cornwall in 1497, trying to lead an army against Henry VII. Henry was merciful. He even let the captive Perkin stay at his royal court. But after two escape attempts Perkin was finally executed. His royal widow married three more times.

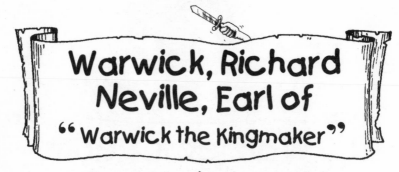

Warwick, Richard Neville, Earl of
"Warwick the Kingmaker"

Powerful nobleman of the Wars of the Roses

1428-71

The Wars of the Roses* (1455-85) were fought between the noble families of York and Lancaster. In the first half of the war, Warwick the Kingmaker was so powerful that his help could make or unmake kings. His kingmaking started in 1461 when he sided with the future Yorkist king, **Edward IV,** to force the feeble

Lancastrian king, **Henry VI,** from the throne. For the next three years Warwick was the most powerful man in the country.

Then Edward and Warwick fell out. Warwick fled to France (1470). There he made it up with Henry VI's wife Margaret of Anjou. (He had to kneel down for fifteen minutes first and apologize to her for what he'd done to her husband.) When Warwick returned to England, he took Henry from the Tower of London, drove Edward into exile - and popped Henry back on the throne!

Edward returned to England in 1471. He defeated and killed Warwick at the Battle of Barnet, fought in a thick mist on 14 April, Easter Sunday. Poor, feeble Henry VI was murdered shortly after.

Watt, James

Clever inventor, once said to have 'invented' the steam engine

1736-1819

A 'watt' is the name of a unit of power. For instance, light bulbs are mostly either 100 watt, 60 watt or 40 watt. The watt is named after James Watt, the Scottish engineer who developed the steam engine.

Watt trained as an instrument maker. In 1764 he was
asked to repair a **Newcomen** steam engine. He thought

he could improve on the design. Steam engines work by producing a vacuum when steam condenses to water. Up to that time a single chamber had to be repeatedly cooled to condense the steam, then heated again for the next lot of steam. Watt developed a new engine which had two chambers, one hot for steam and another cool for condensing it. This was far more efficient. His engines were also the first to power a circular movement so they could drive most kinds of factory machines. By 1800 there were at least 500 of his engines in British factories. They literally powered the industrial revolution and so changed the world. No wonder the 'watt' is named after him.

Wellesley, Arthur, Iˢᵗ Duke of Wellington

Victor of the Battle of Waterloo and inventor of the Wellington boot

1769-1852

Arthur Wellesley is famous for inventing the Wellington boot - and for defeating Napoleon Bonaparte.

He commanded the 'Peninsular' army in Spain during the Napoleonic War, His soldiers were some of the toughest in the world and with them he drove the French invaders out of Spain in a long and bloody campaign (1808-14). His greatest victory was at the Battle of Waterloo (1815), when he defeated the cream of the French army. That was the only time he fought Napoleon face to face. He felt little joy in his victory, mainly sadness over the loss of 15,000 of his men. At his suggestion a medal was given to all ranks who had fought, not just to officers - the first time this was done. It was in the campaign before this victory that he came up with the final design for his famous boot.

Having already been made Duke of Wellington in 1814, he was now the most famous man in Britain. In 1828 he was chosen to be Prime Minister. He continued as the grand old man of British politics (and a very old-fashioned one, it has to be said) almost until his death.

Wellington, Duke of *see above* **Wellesley, Arthur**

Wells, HG (Herbert George)

He wrote *The Time Machine*

1866-1946

HG Wells was short and plump with a high-pitched voice. He was always getting into arguments with fellow socialists* such as **George Bernard Shaw**. He was also very kind, a brilliant talker and one of the most successful writers of his day. Among the hundred or so books which he wrote were: *The Time Machine* (one of the first science fiction books in English), *Love and Mr Lewisham* and *Kipps*.

199

Wesley, John

Energetic founder of Methodism

1703-91

John Wesley was the first leader of the Methodists, a breakaway movement from the Church of England. They were called 'Methodists' after a religious discussion group, started by his brother and helper Charles in Oxford in 1729 (also called the 'Holy Club'). The very first Methodist chapel was built in Bristol ten years later.

John himself never wanted to break away from the Church of England. It was the Church of England which shut its doors on him - because he was too 'enthusiastic'. He was also very energetic. During his life he is said to have preached at least 40,000 sermons and travelled 250,000 miles. Huge crowds of up to 30,000 people would wait for hours to hear him. He was always on the go, even using his travel time to read as he rode. Mostly he preached in working class towns and villages which is why Methodism is most common in working class areas.

Wilberforce, William

Anti-slavery campaigner

1759-1833

William Wilberforce was a wealthy man and a member of Parliament. He was a friend of Prime Minister **William Pitt the Younger**. As such he was just the man to lead a campaign for the abolition of slavery in Britain (started 1787). The first big success came in 1807 when Britain abolished all trade in slaves in its West Indian colonies. (There had been no slaves in Britain itself for many years.) However, slaves who were already slaves stayed that way.

186

From 1821, Wilberforce worked tirelessly for the freeing of all slaves. The Slavery Abolition Act was passed in Parliament just a month after he died. Because Britain was such a powerful country at that time, the British campaign led the way for the abolition of slavery in most parts of the world.

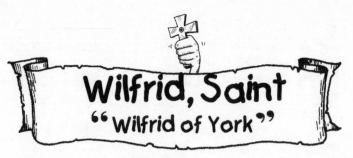

Wilfrid, Saint
"Wilfrid of York"

Saxon bishop who was good at arguing

634-709

Wilfrid was a Saxon bishop. In his day there were two types of Christianity in Britain: Celtic Christianity and Roman Christianity. The Celtic Church had been cut off from the rest of Europe by barbarian invasions at the fall of the Roman Empire (around 400-50). Celtic monks had a different haircut (called a 'tonsure') to other monks and Celtic Christians celebrated Easter on a different date to everyone else. Wilfrid spoke for the Roman Christians at a big debate between the two sides, called the 'Synod of Whitby' (664). He won the debate and from that day Easter was celebrated on the 'Roman' date all over Britain - although haircuts stayed different for some time to come.

Wilkes, John
"Friend of liberty"

Popular politician

1725-97

John Wilkes was hideously ugly and had a bad squint. He was also very good fun and could charm the hind leg off a horse. In his youth he was one of the Medmenham Monks, otherwise known as the Hellfire Club, a group of wild young gentlemen who met at Medmenham Abbey, home of Sir Francis Dashwood. He always spent money like water, hoping that things would turn out right in the end.

In 1762 he started a paper, the *North Briton*, which attacked the Government. The Government tried to silence him and from then on Wilkes became known as a champion of liberty, in particular of the freedom for newspapers to publish what they wanted to. Twice expelled from Parliament although an MP, once imprisoned in the Tower of London, once rescued from arrest by a crowd shouting 'Wilkes and Liberty', once Lord Mayor of London, once wounded in a duel - his life was one long battle, mainly against whatever government was in power. He died as he lived - in debt.

William I
" the Conqueror "

Norman nobleman who conquered England

around 1028-1087, KING OF ENGLAND (NORMAN)

William's father was Robert Duke of Normandy and his mother was a tanner's daughter. (A tanner turns animal skins into leather.) When Robert died in 1035 (William was seven), the Norman nobles didn't want the son of a tanner's daughter to rule them. In the troubled times which followed three of his guardians were killed and his tutor, Osbern, was murdered in front of him. Young William grew up fast - and tough.

74   In 1051 it seems that **Edward the Confessor**, the Saxon king of England may have promised that William would be the next king of England. And in 1064/5
109   **Harold Godwinsson**, the future successor to Edward, may also have promised to support William's claim to the throne. But after Edward died in 1066, the English nobles chose Harold to be king after all. William invaded England to claim the crown and defeated Harold at the Battle of Hastings, perhaps the most important battle ever fought on English soil. William was crowned King of England in Westminster Abbey on Christmas Day 1066. Saxon England was finished.

William was a ruthless but careful ruler. In 1086, to make sure that he knew what his new kingdom was worth, he ordered a survey to be made of all England. This survey, known as the Domesday Book, is one of the most important of all British historical documents.

William died at Rouen in Normandy the following year. He'd grown fat. His body had rotted and burst open in its coffin by the time it was buried in Caen. A horrible stink filled the church.

William II
" Rufus "

Brutal Norman bully

around **1056-1100, KING OF ENGLAND (NORMAN)**

When **William the Conqueror** died in 1087, he left his dukedom of Normandy to his eldest son Robert and his kingdom of England to his middle son William, known as 'Rufus' (Latin for red), due to his red face. William II ruled England for thirteen years. During that time he forced the King of Scotland to submit, conquered Wales and wrestled control of Normandy from his brother. He was a brutal man and made himself 'loathsome to wellnigh all his people,' as one writer puts it.

He was killed by an arrow in the back while hunting in the New Forest. This may well have been murder, arranged by his younger brother the future **Henry I**. William was buried in Winchester Cathedral without a funeral service. No bells were rung to mourn his death.

William III, of Orange

Long-nosed Protestant hero

**1650-1702, KING OF GREAT BRITAIN (JOINTLY WITH HIS
WIFE AS WILLIAM AND MARY) (HOUSE OF STUART)**

William III was a Dutchman (also Prince of the tiny state
of Orange in France - hence William of Orange). In 1671
he was chosen to be ruler, or 'Stadtholder', of
Protestant* Holland after driving out an army of the
Catholic* French King Louis XIV. From then on William
was the champion of Protestant Europe.

151,
129

In 1677, he married **Mary**, daughter of the future King
James II of Britain. James was a Catholic. After James
came to the throne he made himself so unpopular with
his Protestant subjects that they asked William to take
over. In the 'Glorious Revolution' of 1688 William
landed with an army in Devon and James fled the
country. Soon William and his wife were joint rulers of
Britain. William swooped on Catholic opposition in
Scotland and Ireland in the following months (the
Battles of Killicrankie and the Boyne) then spent the rest
of his life ruling Britain and fighting the schemes of
Louis XIV for Catholic control of Europe.

William was thin, clever and brave with a long nose.
When he died, after his horse tripped on a molehill at
Hampton Court, his body was found to contain an
unusually small amount of blood.

William the Lion

Difficult neighbour

1143-1214, KING OF SCOTLAND

Like all medieval Scottish kings, William's biggest problem was always his powerful English neighbour to the south. In 1165, he joined the sons of **Henry II** of England in a rebellion against their father, but was captured by Henry and had to promise allegiance to the English crown. When Henry died in 1189, William bought freedom from this promise by a payment of 10,000 marks to the new English King, **Richard I**. However, by the end of his life, he had once more promised some sort of allegiance to the English crown.

115

194

Wolfe, James

Brave soldier who captured Quebec

1727-59

Late in 1758, **William Pitt** asked James Wolfe to command an expedition against the French colony of Quebec, in modern Canada. At the time the Seven Years

50

War (1756-73) was raging and France and Britain were on opposite sides.

Wolfe crossed the Atlantic and sailed up the Saint Lawrence River. He landed his force opposite Quebec in June the next year. The French held out for a month. In September Wolfe led his troops in a dawn attack. They climbed a steep cliff about a mile upstream from Quebec and forced the French into a surprise battle. Both the French general, the Marquis de Montcalm, and Wolfe were killed. Wolfe died smiling. He knew that he'd won.

Wollstonecraft, Mary

Early campaigner for women's rights
1759-97

Mary Wollstonecraft was a free spirit if ever there was one. She fought for the rights of women at a time when such a thing was almost unheard of, publishing *Thoughts on the Education of Daughters* in 1786 and *A Vindication of the Rights of Women* in 1792, which shocked even her own sisters. That year she went to Paris to see the French Revolution, fell in love with an American and lived with him openly (she didn't believe in marriage). The American was a rat, he left her for other women. In 1796, Mary tried to kill herself by jumping off Putney Bridge in London but she was saved by a passing boat.

She then lived with William Godwin who was almost as

much of a rebel as she was. Neither of them believed in marriage, but they married anyway when she got pregnant - for the sake of the child. Sadly, Mary died while giving birth to the future Mary Shelley. At least she and William had one happy year together.

Wolsey, Thomas, "Cardinal Wolsey"

Lavish Lord Chancellor of Henry VIII

around 1475-1530

120

Thomas Wolsey was the son of an Ipswich butcher who rose to be Lord Chancellor under King **Henry VIII**. From 1515-29 he ruled like a second king. He became very rich and built himself Hampton Court Palace.

41, 24

By 1528, Henry wanted to be rid of his current wife **Catherine of Aragon** so as to be able to marry **Anne Boleyn** - but he had to ask the Pope for permission first, because at that time the English Church was part of the Roman Catholic* Church. Wolsey was a cardinal, an important Catholic churchman, so Henry expected Wolsey to be able to fix things for him. Wolsey failed.

Wolsey fell from power. He died while travelling from York to London under arrest for high treason. Almost his last words were: 'If I had served God as diligently as I have done the King, he would not have given me over in my grey hairs.'

Wordsworth, William

Romantic poet of hills and fields

1770-1850

The poetry of eighteenth century Britain was all thought and no feeling (well, not a lot of feeling). No wonder that by the end of the century some poets were ready for a change. *Lyrical Ballads* (published 1798) was a collection of poems written by two young friends, Samuel Taylor Coleridge and William Wordsworth, who were among the first English Romantic poets. The young Romantics wanted more feeling and less thought, they believed in the power of nature and in simple everyday language. *Lyrical Ballads* started a revolution in English poetry.

Wordsworth saw nature as 'the mind of God'. For much of his life he lived in the Lake District with his beloved sister Dorothy and his wife and children. He loved to walk in the hills. Some of his best poems, such as *I wandered lonely as a cloud*, record simple everyday things. When he was young, he supported the French Revolution, but in later life he became more stodgy in his ideas and his poetry. In 1843 he was made Poet Laureate, official poet to Queen **Victoria**.

223

Wren, Sir Christopher

1632-1723, ARCHITECT

Sir Christopher was a a founder member of the Royal Society*. He designed St Paul's Cathedral, after the old St Paul's burned down in the Fire of London in 1666. He also helped to design fifty-two other London churches mainly with money from a special tax on coal.

Wycliffe, John

Religious reformer
around 1330-1384

John Wycliffe wanted to reform the Medieval Church. Like the later Protestants*, he thought that people should base their religious beliefs on what they read in the Bible, rather than putting all their trust in what priests told them. He had the Bible translated into English, doing some of the work himself, and started a movement of 'poor preachers' to spread his ideas around the country. His followers were called Lollards (from a Dutch word meaning 'mumbler'). After his death, a Lollard uprising led by Sir John Oldcastle was defeated by **Henry V**.

117

His ideas spread across Europe to Bohemia, where John Huss led a major reform movement from 1402.

Glossary

CATHOLICS: Catholics are members of the Roman Catholic Church and the Pope is their leader. Nearly everyone in Western Europe was a Catholic until the early sixteenth century. That was when Protestants broke away. They were fed up with the Catholic Church. In particular, they wanted to read the Bible in their own languages and they thought the Church was too rich and corrupt. Catholics saw the breakaway as a crime against God. Bitter wars of religion followed. England was the most powerful Protestant country facing up to the Catholic powers.

CONSERVATIVES: *see* TORIES

CRUSADES: The eight crusades (1095-1270) were a series of military Christian expeditions to Palestine intended to win control of Jerusalem from the Muslims. The most successful crusade was the first one (1095-99), when Jerusalem was captured and crusader states were set up in the area. By 1187, the Muslims, under their brilliant leader Saladin, had recaptured the city. Further crusades failed to win it back.

DEMOCRACY: A state governed by the elected representatives of the people. There have been continuous, if limited, forms of democracy in England for longer than in any other major country, which is why the British Parliament is called the 'Mother of Parliaments'.

LABOUR PARTY: Originally called the Labour Representation Committee, the Labour Party was formed in 1900 with the backing of the trade unions (set up by workers to fight poverty and bad working conditions). Many trades unionists didn't feel that they were properly listened to within the Liberal Party. The Labour Party aimed to make Britain a better place for working class people to live in.

LIBERAL PARTY: *see* **WHIG**

PAGANS: When Christianity took hold of the Roman Empire, people living in more remote areas clung to the old beliefs of their ancestors. 'Pagan' comes from the Latin *paganus*, meaning a country bumpkin. The word came to be used for followers of all pre-Christian religions in Europe (and later of non-Christians around the world).

PHILANTHROPISTS: The word philanthropist means a lover of human beings. Philanthropists do good for their fellow men and women. The world is a better place for their efforts.

POPE: The head of the Roman Catholic Church, based in the Vatican Palace in Rome.

PROTESTANTS: During the Middle Ages the Roman Catholic Church, based in Rome and led by the Pope, was the only church in Western Europe. By the early sixteenth century this Catholic Church had become corrupt. Priests and monks grew fat on gifts and taxes from the people. A German monk, Martin Luther (1483-1546), started the Reformation to try to reform the Church. All kinds of breakaway movements followed, especially in Northern Europe. The breakaway churches refused to obey the Pope and their followers became known as Protestants. For two hundred years the struggle between the Catholics and Protestants lay behind most European wars.

PUBLIC SCHOOLS: Fee-paying schools, mostly established in the nineteenth century. Really private schools, but called 'public' because the students were not taught by private tutors.

PURITANS: Puritan was a name given to extreme English Protestants in the sixteenth century. They disliked anything in worship which reminded them of Catholicism or 'Popery', such as incense, priests' robes, bishops, religious statues and Catholics.

QUAKERS: The (Religious) Society of Friends, also known as the Quakers was founded in England in the 1640s by George Fox. Quakers were extreme Puritans (see above). They didn't believe in fighting wars, in social classes, in priests, churches or set ways of worshipping God. 'Dissenters' such as Quakers who were outside the Church of England, weren't allowed in government or the universities. They turned to trade. This is why so many great British companies were founded by Quakers, for example, Cadbury's Chocolate.

REPUBLICANS: Republicans believe that countries should be run by the people or for the people, and not by unelected monarchs.

ROYAL SOCIETY: The Royal Society of London for the Promotion of Natural Knowledge, to give it its full name, was granted a royal charter by **Charles II** in 1662. It grew from the Invisible College founded in 1645 by **Robert Boyle** (see page 27) among others. The Royal Society became the most important scientific society in Britain and is internationally famous.

SOCIALISTS: Socialism is the political idea that factories and other ways of making wealth should be controlled by everyone - by society - not just by a small group of rich manufacturers and merchants. That way, so the theory goes, wealth will be shared more evenly and everyone will be happier. Socialists are people who believe in socialism.

STUARTS: Originally *stewards* to the king of Scotland, the Stuarts became the royal family of Scotland from 1371. When **James I/VI** became King of both Scotland and England in 1603, they became the royal family of England as well - until booted out in the Glorious Revolution of 1688.

TORIES: 'Tory' was originally a rude name for an Irish Catholic outlaw. It was thrown at British supporters of the future (Catholic) **James II** in 1689 (see page 129) by his Protestant enemies, who wanted to stop him succeeding to the throne. Later 'Tories' became firm supporters of the Church of England. The 'Tory Party' developed gradually from these confused beginnings during the eighteenth century. By the nineteenth century it had turned into the modern Conservative Party.

WARS OF THE ROSES: The Wars of the Roses are horribly complicated. For thirty years (1455-85) on and off, two families with royal blood battled it out for the crown of England. On one side was the House of Lancaster, symbol a white rose, on the other side was the House of York, symbol a red rose: thus the name Wars of the Roses. Both sides claimed the crown by descent from King **Edward III** (page 77).

WHIG: Whig is Scottish gaelic for a 'horse thief'. It became a rude name for Scottish Protestants. Then in 1689 it was thrown at the powerful English Protestants who wanted to stop or 'exclude' the (Catholic) future **James II** from the throne. They succeeded in stopping him and for the next fifty years Britain was mainly governed by Whig noblemen. By the nineteenth century, the 'Whigs' had developed into the Liberal Party, ancestor of the modern Labour and Liberal (Social Democratic) parties.

British Prime Ministers

Sir Robert Walpole (W)	1721-42	Benjamin Disraeli (Con)	1868
Earl of Wilmington (W)	1742-43	William Gladstone (Lib)	1868-74
Henry Pelham (W)	1743-54	Benjamin Disraeli (Con)	1874-80
Duke of Newcastle (W)	1754-56	William Gladstone (Lib)	1880-85
Duke of Devonshire (W)	1756-57	Marquess of Salisbury (Con)	1885-86
Duke of Newcastle (W)	1757-62	William Gladstone (Lib)	1886
Earl of Bute (T)	1762-63	Marquess of Salisbury (Con)	1886-92
George Grenville (W)	1763-65	William Gladstone (Lib)	1892-94
Marquess of		Earl of Rosebery (Lib)	1894-95
Rockingham (W)	1765-66	Marquess of Salisbury (Con)	1895-1902
Earl of Chatham		Arthur Balfour (Con)	1902-05
(Pitt the Elder) (W)	1766-67	Sir Henry Campbell	
Duke of Grafton (W)	1767-70	-Bannerman (Lib)	1905-08
Lord North (T)	1770-82	Herbert Asquith (Lib)	1908-15
Marquess of		Herbert Asquith (Cln)	1915-16
Rockingham (W)	1782	David Lloyd-George (Cln)	1916-22
Earl of Shelbourne (W)	1782-83	Andrew Bonar Law (Con)	1922-23
Duke of Portland Cln)	1783	Stanley Baldwin (Con)	1923-24
William Pitt		James Ramsay	
(the Younger) (T)	1783-1801	Macdonald (Lab)	1924
Henry Addington (T)	1801-04	Stanley Baldwin (Con)	1924-29
William Pitt		James Ramsay	
(the Younger) (T)	1804-06	Macdonald (Lab)	1929-31
Lord Grenville (W)	1806-07	James Ramsay	
Duke of Portland (T)	1807-09	Macdonald (Cln)	1931-35
Spencer Percival (T)	1809-12	Stanley Baldwin (Cln)	1935-37
Earl of Liverpool (T)	1812-27	Neville Chamberlain (Cln)	1937-40
George Canning (T)	1827	Winston Churchill (Cln)	1940-45
Viscount Goderich (T)	1827-28	Winston Churchill (Con)	1945
Duke of Wellington (T)	1828-30	Clement Attlee (Lab)	1945-51
Earl Grey (W)	1830-34	Sir Winston Churchill (Con)	1951-55
Viscount Melbourne (W)	1834	Sir Anthony Eden (Con)	1955-57
Sir Robert Peel (T)	1834-35	Harold Macmillan (Con)	1957-63
Viscount Melbourne (W)	1835-41	Sir Alec Douglas-Home (Con)	1963-64
Sir Robert Peel (T)	1841-46	Harold Wilson (Lab)	1964-70
Lord John Russell (W)	1846-52	Edward Heath (Con)	1970-74
Earl of Derby (T)	1852	Harold Wilson (Lab)	1974-76
Earl of Aberdeen (Plt)	1852-55	James Callaghan (Lab)	1976-79
Viscount Palmerston (Lib)	1855-58	Margaret Thatcher (Con)	1979-90
Earl of Derby (Con)	1858-59	John Major (Con)	1990-97
Viscount Palmerston (Lib)	1859-65	Tony Blair (Lab)	1997-2007
Earl Russell (Lib)	1865-66	Gordon Brown (Lab)	2007-10
Earl of Derby (Con)	1866-68	David Cameron (Con)	2010-

PARTY CODES   Coalition - (Cln); Conservative - (Con); Liberal - (Lib); Labour - (Lab); Peelite - (Plt); Tory - (T); Whig - (W).

British monarchs

Monarchs of England
(up to 1603)

SAXONS

Egbert	827-839
Æthelwulf	839-858
Æthelbald	858-860
Æthelbert	860-865
Æthelred I	865-871
Alfred the Great	871-899
Edward the Elder	899-924
Æthelstan	924-939
Edmund	939-946
Edred	946-955
Edwy	955-959
Edgar	959-975
Edward the Martyr	975-978
Æthelred the Unready	978-1016
Edmund Ironside	1016

DANES

Canute	1016-1035
Harold I Harefoot	1035-1040
Harthacnut	1040-1042

SAXONS

Edward the Confessor	1042-1066
Harold II	1066

NORMANS

William the Conqueror	1066-1087
William II	1087-1100
Henry I	1100-1135
Stephen	1135-1154

PLANTAGENETS

Henry II	1154-1189
Richard I	1189-1199
John	1199-1216
Henry III	1216-1272
Edward I	1272-1307
Edward II	1307-1327
Edward III	1327-1377
Richard II	1377-1399

HOUSE OF LANCASTER

Henry IV	1399-1413
Henry V	1413-1422
Henry VI	1422-1461

HOUSE OF YORK

Edward IV	1461-1483
Edward V	1483
Richard III	1483-1485

TUDORS

Henry VII	1485-1509
Henry VIII	1509-1547
Edward VI	1547-1553
Mary I	1553-1558
Elizabeth I	1558-1603

Scotland was a unified, independent kingdom (off and on) throughout the Middle Ages. In 1603 **James VI** of Scotland became King of England as well, although the two countries were still separate. They were finally united in the Acts of Union (1707). Wales and Ireland on the other hand

British monarchs

Monarchs of Scotland
(up to 1603)

Malcolm II	1005-1034
Duncan I	1034-1040
Macbeth	1040-1057
Malcolm II (Canmore)	1058-1093
Donald Bane	1093-1094
Duncan II	1094
Donald Bane	1094-1097
Edgar	1097-1107
Alexander I	1107-1124
David I	1124-1153
Malcolm IV	1153-1165
William the Lion	1165-1214
Alexander II	1214-1249
Alexander III	1249-1286
Margaret of Norway	1286-1290
No one at all	1290-1292
John Balliol	1292-1296
No one at all	1296-1306
Robert I (Bruce)	1306-1329
David II	1329-1371

STUARTS

Robert II	1371-1390
Robert III	1390-1406
James I	1406-1437
James II	1437-1460
James III	1460-1488
James IV	1488-1513
James V	1513-1542
Mary	1542-1567
James VI (also became James I of England from 1603)	1567-1625

Monarchs of Britain
(1603 - present)

STUARTS

James I/VI	1603-1625
Charles I	1625-1649

COMMONWEALTH

No monarchs	1649-1660
(Dominated by Oliver Cromwell)	

STUARTS

Charles II	1660-1685
James II/VII	1685-1688
William III (jointly) }	1689-1702
Mary II (jointly) }	1689-1694
Anne	1702-1714

HOUSE OF HANOVER

George I	1714-1727
George II	1727-1760
George III	1760-1820
George IV	1820-1830
William IV	1830-1837
Victoria	1837-1901

HOUSE OF SAXE-COBURG

Edward VII	1901-1910

WINDSORS

George V	1910-1936
Edward VIII	1936
George VI	1936-1952
Elizabeth II	1952-present

were never unified, independent kingdoms for any length of time. Wales was subject to the English crown by the thirteenth century. Ireland was colonised and controlled by England with varying success from Norman times until independence in the twentieth century.

Index

Published in 2014 by Wayland
Text and illustrations copyright Bob Fowke 2014

Wayland
33 Euston Road
London NW1 3BH

Produced for Wayland by Bob Fowke & Co
Cover design: Lisa Peacock
Cover illustration: Miguel Francisco

A CIP catalogue record for this book is available from the British Library

ISBN 978 0 7502 8156 0

10 9 8 7 6 5 4 3 2 1

Printed and bound by Clays Ltd, St Ives plc

First published in 2000 by Hodder Children's Books

Wayland is a division of Hachette Children's Books, an Hachette company
www.hachette.co.uk